Drugs to Riches

by Frank Marino

Drags to Riche$

Copyright ©
Frank Marino Enterprises
1909 Redbird Drive
Las Vegas, NV 89134
702-363-8361

First Edition   Copyright 2020   Frank Marino
ISBN-13: 978-1986945257
ISBN-10: 1986945251

Follow Me On...

 Frank Marino &
Frank Marino Fan Page &
Frank Marino Divas Las Vegas
 @thequeenofvegas
 @thequeenofvegas
 FrankMarinosDivas

All Rights Reserved: No Part of this book may be reproduced or transmitted in any way, form, or by any means, electronic, mechanical, including photocopying, recording, or by any information storage and retrieval system, without the written permission of the distributor/copyright owner, except where permitted by law.

Photo Credits:
All photos from the Frank Marino collection.

In Loving Memory of
My Three Moms

Sandra Marino

Sarah Paz

Mary Mastrangelo

and of course another type of mother...
Joan Rivers

Table of Contents

1. Goodbye Ms. Rivers 7
2. So Much to Say, So Little Voice 21
3. Who's Your Daddy? 31
4. The Crash of 9/11 41
5. Good Investments Bad People 51
6. My Cherie Amour 59
7. A Fortune in Free Facelifts 67
8. Success is Not for the Lazy 77
9. The Last Day I Was Happy 87
10. The Producer From Hell 97
11. The Death of "La Cage" 105
12. I Wasn't Done Talking 113
13. The Birth of "Divas!" 117
14. The 20 Year Itch 133
15. With Great Love Comes Great Loss 151
16. Knocking Down My Playground 163
17. The Showboy Mansion 173
18. Reality Hits! 191
19. Baby and Angel 201
20. Embezzled, Extorted and Exonerated 209
21. Comeback is Better Than the Setback 227

Goodbye Ms. Rivers

It was just three days before Joan Rivers died, the first of September 2014. I remember lying in my bed trying to wake up and looking over the many emails I always get on my phone. My boyfriend, Alex, had come into the room. I knew something bad was about to come out of his mouth by the stunned look on his face.

"Frank," he told me gently. "Joan Rivers is apparently in a coma."

I realize now, I must have gone into shock because I kept talking about how I needed to get to the gym and what appointments I had on my

schedule for the day. My brain just couldn't take it in or accept what he was trying to tell me. **Joan for me, was forever and as far back as I could remember, always such a huge part of my life.**

"Frank, calm down," Alex told me, but I was not having it. Routine, I needed routine. I went about doing all the trivial things that always start my day. I continued to go over my appointments, brushed my teeth, got dressed — Anything to keep from thinking about what Alex was saying.

"She had apparently gone in for a medical procedure to have her throat examined, because her voice was sounding raspy when she was performing on stage." Alex kept trying to get through to me. "Frank, are you hearing me?"

I was hearing him, but I didn't want to listen. Part of my mind was totally focused on what Alex was saying but the rest of it was running in the other direction. Alex's tone was so serious and yet so gentle. With all the years we've been together, Alex knows me better than anyone else. He knew at that moment to wait for my mind to catch up. And then it did. I just slumped onto the edge of the bed in complete shock. Medical procedure? Raspy throat? After all I'd been through with my voice (which I'll explain later), I could understand her concern, **BUT IN A COMA?** How the Hell did this happen?

At first, I couldn't stay still and had to know what was going on. We went online to find out what had actually happened. I then turned on the television and noticed that it was all over the news both the local and national media began calling me as well. Geraldo, Dateline, and 20/20 were asking me for interviews. I agreed to do all of them. Within a two day period, **I must have been on 20 different television programs discussing what Joan Rivers meant to me, my life, and my career.** Even in my state of shock, I was able to find the strength to get through the emotional drain that it had taken on me to discuss the love I have for a woman who I so much admire and respect.

Apparently, the day earlier she was doing a book signing for her latest autobiography. That same night she was trying out some new comedy material in a small club in Greenwich Village, and was scheduled to perform at the Borgata Hotel in Atlantic City the following day after her procedure. I've had enough experience with doctors to know that if she had a performance scheduled the next day, **the doctors must have told her that this procedure would be an "in-and-out" thing** and there should be no complications. I know this because both Joan and I were very similar in our work ethics.

On the News Finally Realizing That I Won't Be Able to Keep up With the "Joans'" Anymore

At this point, Joan and I had come full circle together. It was Joan who had introduced me to the producer of the show "An Evening at La Cage," Lou Paciocco, where I had landed my first job in the business. I'd studied and impersonated Joan on stage for over 35 years. **She'd even sued me in 1986 for five million dollars (thank God we settled, I was like eight bucks short) something that might have broken lesser relationships. But not ours. We reconciled our differences and the relationship became even stronger.** (For that whole juicy story get my first book, *His Majesty, the Queen*.)

We became such close friends that she invited me on all of her talk shows (both daytime and prime time) and she even called me in to do an episode of "E! Fashion Police" just before she passed.

"Can We Talk" It's Miss Joan Rivers

On "E! Fashion Police" With Joan Rivers

I appeared on her daytime talk show so many times we both lost count. Once, on her late night show, I won a Joan look-alike contest against fifty women and over one hundred drag queens.

She had become so incredibly supportive of my career that she'd be on TV promoting a product and bring my name up. She'd talk about how I was getting plastic surgery to look more like her and she was getting so much plastic surgery to look less like her that she might end up looking like me!

On "E! Fashion Police" they were doing a big story on what she would wear to a celebrity wedding and she had me come out impersonating her in a gown that she would have worn to Jennifer Aniston's wedding, if she'd been invited.

When she introduced me to the audience, she said, "I've been friends with Frank Marino for over 35 years, he's the world's best female impersonator. In that time, I don't know what's been tucked more, my face or his penis," which I thought was perfectly clever and funny.

From as far back as I can remember I'd always loved Joan, and over the years she'd given me some of the best advice in the business. She was more than a role model to me; she was like a fourth mother, of which I've already had three (Sandra, Sarah, and Mary).

Later, I found out from the news that the doctors had apparently taken selfies with Joan while she was under anesthesia. This was a horrible violation of every rule of medical ethics and human behaviour! It never ceases to amaze me how people can be so unprofessional and expect not to ever get called out. **That is why I always say celebrities don't start out being "Divas," it's this industry that makes them become that way.**

I always say that if you abuse a small puppy enough, you'll eventually get bitten. Anger builds within celebrities when they are mistreated. Remember, the public most often only sees the good things in our careers. They don't get to see all the things that fall through the cracks or the rejection. That's why many entertainers say they would not want their children to go into the business. They just don't want to see them being rejected.

So, apparently, something went wrong at the surgery center. They found something in her throat and removed a piece of it to do a biopsy. It turned out that she stopped breathing during the procedure for around eight minutes. Because they were unable to get her to the hospital in time, she ended up in a coma for a couple of days which must have been torture for her daughter, Melissa.

My own mothers' deaths (I'll explain later) took a huge toll on me. I spent years wanting to do nothing more than sleep, because while dreaming, my mother was still alive. **I knew exactly what Melissa was going through. I felt so sympathetic for her, as my own heart was breaking as well.**

All of this kept me in a state of complete disbelief. No one would notice from watching the interviews, but inside I was a total wreck. It wasn't the first time and it probably wouldn't be the last time that I'd be forced to go on stage with a broken heart and do my job of making people laugh much like I'm sure, Joan Rivers herself had certainly done many times.

Not a day in the last 35 years has the name Joan Rivers hadn't come up in my household at least six or seven times. **She is such a big part of my life!** Here was a woman whose career enabled to support two households very, very well, a joke Joan would remind me of every time I was with her.

I was extremely honored to be invited to her funeral in Manhattan and Shiva at Melissa's house in Pacific Palasades, California. (Shiva is a Jewish tradition when a family member dies.) It's one thing for me to know that Joan and I were close, and touching that Melissa understood our connection as well.

Unfortunately, with my seven-day-a-week "Divas" show schedule, I couldn't make it to the funeral in New York, but I did attend the Shiva at Melissa's house. I remember when

Me and Sandra on the Red Carpet for Miss Congeniality 2

I stepped out of the car with my plate of cookies, my showbiz professionalism (or shall I say my ego) was at war with my grief. Normally when faced with the paparazzi, who were everywhere, I'd usually pose, smile and make a quip, but not here, not at Joan's Shiva. **It would have been wrong to pose for a picture.** Not since the red carpet premiere of "Miss Congeniality 2" with Sandra Bullock had I experienced anything like that with hundreds of cameras going off, practically blinding me.

Once inside, I was sitting there on Melissa's pristine ivory couch surrounded by all the people who loved Joan. Her photos were up everywhere, and people were talking about her as if she was sitting amoung us. Alex sat next to me holding my hand but it felt like a dream; nothing felt real! The woman I idolized for so many years was no longer with us. **At that surreal moment, comedy legends Don Rickles, Lily**

Tomlin, and Steve Lawrence walked up to me and gave their condolences because each of these stars know what Joan means to me. They were all so kind to me during our period of grief. For the first time ever I actually started to feel old because I had known these legends for so long but had to be introduced to the newest stars of today, like the Kardashians.

I remember talking to Kris Jenner about MacKenzie-Childs' home products that we both have in our kitchens. I could always spot them when I watched the reality show Keeping Up with the Kardashians. Chris also joked with me that Joan was the first celebrity to bump their family off the cover of People with her death. Kim Kardashian and I had previously met once at a function for the opening of Pink's Hot Dogs in Las Vegas, but that was long before I knew that Bruce Jenner, her step-father, would have a sex change operation and become Caitlyn Jenner. Who knew that in years to come we'd have so much more in common than we thought at the time?

I also found out some other interesting things at the Shiva.

Me with Kim Kardashian

Frank Marino

Catching Up On Caitlyn Jenner

Page 16

Like myself, Joan Rivers was extremely vain, but I don't consider that a bad thing! I was impressed to hear that Melissa did something that I would like someone to do for me as well (if I ever ended up in a similar situation). As we all know Joan as the Chief of the Fashion Police, always dressed impeccably whenever she left the house. So since all the paparazzi were attempting to capture pictures of Joan in the hospital, Melissa decided to dress her in a beautiful gown with hair and makeup as if she was about to perform on stage. When visitors came, Joan was ready to receive them. Thank God for family members who know what you need when you can't do certain things for yourself! I was extremely touched by the dignity Melissa gave her mother, especially in her final days.

I remember telling Melissa that I was considering taking Joan out of my show for a while, out of respect, but she said, "If anyone would want you to keep performing as her, it would be my Mom," Melissa told me with a pat on the back of my hand. Well, that certainly straightened me out about that. She was right of course. Joan would have wanted me to keep her legacy alive. In fact, on her talk show she asked me, **"What are you going to do if I ever die?"** I joked, **"I'll just have to join the show 'Legends in Concert.'"** She laughed and the audience went crazy. It actually got the biggest laugh of the entire show.

From here on in, it's a great honor to keep Joan Rivers' legacy alive. For me, it's no longer an impersonation, it's now a tribute to the funniest woman that ever lived.

As fate would have it when Joan published her latest biography, *Diary of a Mad Diva*, I was approached by a publisher, Trish, to write the next chapters of my story as well. When I

Frank Marino

At the Joan Rivers Dress Museum

finished *His Majesty, the Queen* over 25 years ago, I thought I had done everything I'd set out to do in my life. Boy, was I wrong! There was so much more waiting for me. Things I've always wanted and other things I didn't even realize I wanted. **My goals over the years have changed as I have grown. There's always something more in store for this Diva!**

We were going to reprint *His Majesty, the Queen*, so we started to write a bonus chapter, but there was much more to share. Trish, said that we were going to have to pen another book. What was I going to do? Say no?

To be honest, I didn't want to write another one. The first book was so demanding of me that I ended up getting depressed, rehashing all the memories from my childhood. But when I was sitting on that ivory couch in Melissa's living room, I knew that I had so much more to tell. **So here we go again....**

As One Door Closes, Another One Opens

So Much to Say, So Little Voice

Joan worrying about her voice was something that resonated with me and brought back the worst nightmare of my entire life. It was right after my show's 10 year anniversary in 1995. I'd just finished working on my first book, *His Majesty, the Queen*, when I had actually started to lose my own voice.

As an impersonator my voice is my life — it's what my entire career is all about. When I am on stage as Joan Rivers, she talks very fast and it takes a lot of control of my tongue and vocal chords at that speed to sound like her. Even now, I practice a lot. I speak very fast in these long run-on sentences (like most of this book is written) to make it so I can sound like Joan. I sometimes even use my falsetto voice; it's actually a lot like the strength you need to hold notes when you sing.

For me, it all started with a slight depression, which had come about after rehashing my entire past for my last book and reliving some bad experiences. Now you wouldn't think that depression would cause a person to lose their voice. It didn't. The cure did. I remember feeling sluggish and tired all the time. I'd snap at people for the littlest things. I didn't understand why I was feeling so down; after all I was on top of the world. My career was going well, my romantic life with Alex seemed good, and I had a great new family as well as an old family whom I loved very much. You would think I would have been feeling great.

A doctor told me that depression was uncontrollable. It was an imbalance of serotonin in the brain and that it would have to be regulated. He prescribed a brand-new antidepressant called Paxil. Before going on Paxil I had never taken anything stronger than a baby aspirin because I always seemed the picture of perfect health.

At first, Paxil had a wonderful effect on me. It not only calmed me down, but it also made me able to deal with challenges that before would make me blow up. You could have told me the house burned down and I'd say, "Fine, we'll get another one." If I had not lost my voice, I probably would have been the spokesperson for the drug because it made me feel that good. In the beginning I didn't notice it much, but I slowly started to realize that my words were beginning to slur. **I thought it was all the stress I was under.** I was in the middle of doing a 10 year Anniversary gala of Golden Rainbow (a local Las Vegas charity to help people who have AIDS) and it was during the rehearsals that I noticed that I was slurring my words all the time. I

Performing at Golden Rainbow

thought I was just very tired from doing three shows a night at the hotel and then the benefit rehearsals in the afternoons. At first, I really didn't think anything of it — at least not yet!

But after the Golden Rainbow event was over with, I started to notice that my voice still wasn't right. One sequence of words that I was saying every night in my show would still slur. I'd say, "Where I live, in Beverly Hills." **And I couldn't say Beverly Hills without slurring the words.** Those syllables were formulated in a way that I just couldn't get them to come out of my mouth correctly, like a tongue twister. I tried to find other different ways to change things to cover it up. "Beverly Hills" was hard for me to say, so I took it out and just said, "California," which for me was much easier. It was the first of many little changes in my speech because I kept changing words until I woke up one morning and I couldn't even say my own name. At this point I freaked out! Looking back, we had no idea that it was the new drug Paxil that my doctor had prescribed that was causing this speech impediment.

To give an example of what I sounded like would be a stroke victim trying to regain their voice. **I was in the middle of a 10 year, ten million dollar contract and I could not let anyone know I was experiencing this handicap because then they would have a reason to let me out of my contract.** I didn't tell anyone except Alex, and of course the doctors.

I felt so utterly inadequate! I would go on stage and say that I'd just had dental work that afternoon and the Novocain hadn't worn off yet. I did this so many nights that to this day people will come up to me and say, "I was there on the day you had dental work done." Little did they know, I had "dental work" every day for close to 10 years. Sometimes when I went onstage, saliva would come out of the corners of my mouth. I had to take a dainty lady's handkerchief with me and I would dab ever so slightly to get the spit off my chin or wherever it landed.

People didn't understand it. I started to get notes backstage like, "Is Frank Marino drunk?" and "How could he go on stage like that?" The worst part was that I felt that couldn't tell them the truth! As a matter of fact, I don't drink at all. To this day, I never have. I just never liked the taste so it was extremely humiliating for me, to say the least. My producer probably described it best, and this is probably the only thing I'll ever give him credit for saying it was "like watching a wounded animal." You could be the king of the jungle but if you can't attack your prey, you're just waiting to get attacked yourself. That hit me very hard because he was absolutely correct.

Normally I would help the other performers prepare for their performances, correcting minor mistakes here or there, but I didn't feel like I could do that either. I always expected 100% from everybody but I have never asked for more than what I gave. How could I criticize others when I couldn't speak clearly? I couldn't say to them, maybe try this or try that. Because they would be like, "Worry about fixing your own act before you criticize mine." What they didn't understand was that I had a medical issue that couldn't be instantly fixed.

It's like people who have to carry around an oxygen tank. Every breath is a chore, where the rest of us just take it for granted breathing effortlessly 24-hours a day and not even thinking about it. For me, it was the same way with talking.

Every word I said involved a special thought process. As if that wasn't awful enough, it worsened in the upper register of my voice that I used to impersonate Joan! I felt like I was actually on the verge of losing my entire career.

It was so shameful, and I had to keep it as my little secret. My producer knew about my problem but it was still more cost effective than trying to replace me. So, I was only able to stay at "La Cage" for that reason or I would have been out the door.

Of course, I spent every day searching for an answer. Alex and I knew that I'd never taken any other drugs and since it had started around the time I'd started Paxil, it must be the cause. I immediately stopped taking it after only 3 months. We, of course, hoped it would clear up but even with it out of my system for weeks, it persisted. Even the doctor said, "It can't be Paxil. It's out of your system at this point. It must be something neurological."

The doctors tested me for everything under the sun. First, they thought I had ALS, then Myasthenia Gravis, and after that, Parkinson's disease. If it was a neurological issue, they tested me for it. I went to every medical center that money could buy. And they weren't just the run of the mill doctors. They were the best of the best and because of who I am, I was moved to the front of the line. I took all their tests: x-rays, cat scans, MRIs. I even went to Bethesda, Maryland where they have the military clinic. They flew me there for free because they'd never seen anything like it. I was also seen by the Mayo Clinic, Scripps, and UCLA, who thought it was sinusitis and gave me a nasal operation. I literally went everywhere. **Every doctor came up with a different diagnosis, but in the end, none of them were correct!**

Throughout this process, I continued performing on stage working three shows per night. The way I survived those 10 years of medical challenges was to experiment with different coping mechanisms. For example, I found that if I chewed on a piece of candy, I could lock my jaw into place and talk like a ventriloquist by just moving my tongue. I knew I didn't want all the sugar from the candy 24 hours a day/7 days a week, so I replaced it with a small button. I'd place a button in my mouth between my back teeth and clench onto it. There must

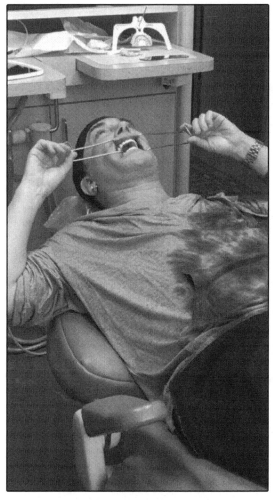

At One of My Many Doctor Appointments

have been at least two or three buttons that I swallowed on stage. Joan Rivers had this, "Oh," sound right before she gets to the grit of something, or as she's remembering something. Only there's this intake of breath after that "Oh," and I'd open my jaw, whoops, and down the little button went. I actually gagged on stage a couple of times.

Frank Marino

The Sign Says It Even If I Can't

There were so many embarrassing moments, I really can't recall them all. Once I was doing this commercial shoot and I couldn't get the words out clearly. It was horrible! They must have thought I was high on drugs! To be someone who has never even tried any kind of drug, it was overwhelming and humiliating. I'd do my best to hide it while on stage because I couldn't bear to lose my job. I wanted the money to continue to live well in the style to which I'd grown accustomed. I certainly didn't want to lose everything I had worked so hard for over the years because of this impediment. But I truly felt like a fraud cheating our audiences, especially when they complimented me after the show. **I knew I would have been so much better if only I could speak fluently again.**

After a while, the buttons started chipping the veneers on my teeth. I couldn't suck on the candy because of the sugar, and now the buttons were creating even more problems. I then moved on to chewing on these small rubber stoppers, the type that you put on the bottom of tabletop items to prevent scratches on your furniture. They also gave me some bounce and slack if I were to bite down too hard. They were soft enough not to chip my teeth and had zero calories. Win-win!

The worst part of this entire nightmare was that when all the medical tests kept coming back negative, they had me thinking that I was crazy, and it was all psychosomatic. There's nothing like being flown all over the country for test after test as a fluke case of the disease of the month only to find out that when those tests come back negative, the doctors look at you sideways and say, "It must be in your head." **Great! I went from being a fluke to a mental patient!**

So, this continued for about 10 years. Ten years of hiding the shame of slurring words. Ten years of utter frustration and humiliation.

I Had to Remain a Success!
I Could Learn to Live
Without Necessities
But Still Wanted the Luxuries

Who's Your Daddy?

Having this medical problem looming over me all the time, and having doctor after doctor tell me that they didn't know what was wrong with me, I began to fear that I was going to die. I drew up my will and got a living trust together. Meanwhile, I started checking off items on my bucket list.

Alex and I traveled every opportunity that we could. **My goal was to visit each Disney park around the world.** This year we're going to the newest one Shanghai Disneyland. We've already enjoyed Disney parks in Tokyo, Paris, Hong Kong, California, and of course Florida, the biggest and grandest of them all.

I just love the way the Disney company is run and the hospitality that they teach their employees to use with every guest. You don't see customer service like that anymore, especially in Las Vegas.

Alex and I Visiting Disney Tokyo

I try to infuse my show with the hospitality that Disney guests get to experience when a person comes to see my "Divas" show. We always strive to make guests feel they are part of our family. I believe the reason my show has continued all these years is because I'm able to update the show and incorporate the newest and hottest music superstars. **My latest addition was to stream live on Facebook prior to every show and allow the audience to choose the stars they would like to see performing that evening.**

Now, for those of you who have read my first book, *His Majesty, the Queen* (which, of course, is available on FrankMarino.com - LOL) you know all about my search for my birth mother Mary. For the rest of you, here's a synopsis: after having a loving relationship with my adoptive mother, Sandra Marino, and then another fabulous relationship with my godmother, Sarah, who took me in when my adoptive parents died, I was fortunate enough to have yet another amazing relationship with my birth mother, Mary. I found out I was adopted when I was eighteen years old and decided to search for her.

With this newfound fear that I might die, I really felt a strong need to finally meet my birth father as well. I utilized the same agency that I had used years prior to find my birth mother. I became such good friends with the woman who had found my birth mother that she would come to see my show in Vegas with her family. Adoption investigation services run between $6,000 and $10,000, but we'd become such good friends that she offered to do the search for my birth father for free.

The original story I got from my birth mother was that she was a young, 16-year-old girl, and my father was about 21 or 22 years old. She told me that she was unaware that he was married and that the first time they had relations, she became pregnant with me. She also said he was very abusive, both verbally and physically to her during the pregnancy because he knew he could have gotten in trouble with the law because she was underage. She said he would hit her and even threatened to push her down the steps and try to kill the baby. Meanwhile, at the same time, his wife was also pregnant.

As it turns out my half-sister, Kim, and I were born one a month apart. She was born in October 1963 and I was born in November 1963. Come to find out, I also have an older half-brother, Jimmy. Both Kim and Jimmy have

My Birth-Father Frank Parker

children, so I'm also an uncle. When my birth father's first marriage failed, he remarried, and he had my half-sisters Shannon and Bridget. So, it turns out that I have a very large family and we, of course, have no idea how many other Frank Marinos are out there!

Unfortunately, when the search was complete, I found out I was four years too late. My birth father, Frank Parker, had died, down-and-out on his luck, four years earlier. I would have liked to have met him and gotten to know a little bit about him. I regret not searching for him sooner.

I wasn't named after Frank Parker, though he didn't name any of his other children after himself either. Coincidentally, Frank Marino, my adopted father, gave me his name, so I became Frank Marino Jr. As fate would have it, I ended up with my birth father's name after all but my adopted father was the only father figure that ever spent time with me, throwing a ball and teaching me how to ride a bike.

There's one thing about finding a long-lost family that I want to make clear. While it's well worth the effort for anyone who's adopted to do so, don't expect to fit in immediately. I was lucky with Mary and I do my best to be a good brother to my half-siblings, but no matter how hard I try, I'll never feel like I entirely belong. **I wasn't there for the sibling squabbles, the family outings, or the Sunday dinners.** The bond from living through those events can't be relived or reproduced. Those endearing feelings don't just pop up because of the blood shared between us, but the bond is still very strong.

The first of my father's family that I met was my half-sister Kim and her husband when they came out to Vegas to see my show. They brought pictures and answers to my hundreds of questions about our father. She was lovely and I noticed a few shared mannerisms here and there that were like mine, which

With My Half-Sister Kim

My Birth-Father and My Half-Brother Jimmy

made me feel some camaraderie. It was strange for me to say "our father." **When I was talking with them, I was always referring to him as her father.** It's taken a long time for me to feel justified to say that he was just as much my biological father as he was hers or any of my other half-siblings.

My birth father's family have been pretty good about it considering that they learned their father had been unfaithful to their mother with a minor. They've tried to accept me, but it feels like they're being polite and sometimes the interaction is a little forced. Everyone is nice to each other because of the situation my father created but, for example, my brother Jimmy would never just pick up a phone and call me and, of course, I understand that.

Frank Parker didn't have the best life. From what I found out, he was a playboy growing up, a womanizer, and a little bit eccentric. **I'm not quite sure what he went through later in life but when he passed, I heard he was broke.** What runs through my head is that if I had met him, could I have helped him? If so, would he have even accepted my help? I definitely would have tried.

I would say I became closest to my father's brother Tom and his wife, Marie who came out to Vegas often and could not have been nicer. They still stay in touch to this day and have given me phone numbers so I could contact other family members. **They introduced me to my other extended family as well and my father's other wife and children.**

Next to Tom and Maria, I felt the closest attachment to my half-sister, Bridget. She was so young when we first met and she loved coming to Vegas. She'd vacation here a lot with her friends for a while and eventually moved here for two years.

I try to stay in touch with all my family. There are a lot of them on both my birth father's and my birth mother's sides. I do my best to stay in touch because I'm not going to lose them again.

The story that my birth father's family tells me about my birth mother is different than what she had told me. They said my birth mother knew very well that he was married and she used to sneak into his house to be with him. My father's sister Ann would even hang out with them sometimes. They say that there are always three sides to every story. His, hers, and the truth which is often somewhere in between the two.

I don't blame my birth mother for putting me up for adoption but must say I felt a little bitter towards my grandparents. These were young children who could have used their parents' help. I'm grateful that my mother didn't get an abortion, but I was always brought up that if you can feed one, you can feed two just as easily. I don't care how poor you are, you could have kept that child. When you put a child up for adoption, you don't know what you're going to put that child through or where they will end up. Yeah, they could have a better life, but they could also have a worse one.

One thing for certain, an adopted child will always feel left out. **Even with the parents I had loving me as much as they did, I've sometimes felt like I just didn't quite fit in.**

I found it very odd that when I went to meet my birth father's family, they were going to bring his mother, my grandmother, but she wasn't feeling well and didn't come. **If it were me, I wouldn't care if I had pneumonia, I'd go to see the grandchild whom I had never met before.** Looking back, there were times that I'd hear stories about my grandfather on my mother's side being so excited when my mother had my half-brother Louis, a boy at last, that my grandfather could play sports with. I felt he already had a boy to play sports with and he made his daughter give him up because of his own shame and embarrassment.

Mary's other child was a girl, Nikki, who I speak with all the time along with her husband Eric. I'm also very close to my nephew Louis, my brother Louis's son. Obviously, I'm closer to them than I am with my birth father's side, but then I've had Mary to pave the way and bridge the gap.

My first parents were the Marinos who adopted me when I was a baby straight out of the hospital. They both passed away from cancer when I was just six and nine years old, and that sad story is in the first book. I was only seven when my godmother, Sarah, took me in. There's no one on this planet that I could ever love more than Sarah. She loved me just as much as her own children and treated me just like I was one of her own, sometimes better.

So with four different families, I should feel like I have the biggest family ever, but I sometimes still feel alone. Maybe that was where my need to be in show business was born because maybe, psychologically, I thought I could surround myself with lots of people and create my own, handpicked family.

Blood is Thicker Than Water

The Crash of 9/11

After meeting my birth father's family, the next big event I started to plan was my mother Sarah's 50th wedding anniversary party, which my brothers and sisters and I threw for them at the beautiful Carlton Reception Hall in Eisenhower Park on Long Island, New York.

I remember buying Sarah the most beautiful champagne-colored lace gown and fabulous jewelry, shoes and accessories to match. I couldn't wait. She was going to look stunning. It was scheduled for September 22, 2001. We were all so excited. It took

Sarah's Lace Dress

us over a year to plan the big event and, as you know, I left no stone unturned from the flowers to the food. This was going to be the best party our family had ever experienced. I spared no expense. All was on track and going great until the morning of September 11, 2001 when I got an unusually early-morning phone call from Sarah telling me, "We're being attacked!"

I immediately got up and turned on the news and I watched, like everyone else around the world. I remember seeing the Twin Towers on fire. Tower one fell. I could not believe what I was seeing. Then the plane went into Tower two and in no time, tower two fell. **I was grabbing my phone and punching in numbers as fast as I could.** I had so many family members and friends who either lived or worked in that area of the city!

The phone lines were down so I couldn't get through. After my mother Sarah called me, it would be hours before I could reach her again. I also kept trying to call my mother Mary and was finally able to get through. Thankfully the entire family was fine.

My half-sister, Kim, was working a block away and saw the whole thing. To this day Kim is traumatized about the entire experience and who wouldn't be? Friends, coworkers and people we all knew had lost friends and loved ones in this unbelievable tragedy.

What I visually saw that day was an attack on America. What I didn't see coming was the attack on the economy. There were thousands of people who no longer had jobs to return to. It all happened so fast. Las Vegas was hit hard because people were focusing on their necessities now, not their luxuries. And **let's face it gambling**

New York State of Mind

and entertainment are luxuries. Maybe people didn't have the extra expendable cash. **We actually went from selling out three shows a night to maybe half that.**

This was the first time that I really was forced to jump into work mode and start doing the television shows and the other things that kept our show in the spotlight. I'd always done these things, but now I *had* to do them.

My Whole Family at Sarah's 50th Anniversary Party

We had so many people who were coming to Sarah's anniversary party who, at the last minute, cancelled, which I didn't understand because **if we have to alter our lives because of a terrorist, then we have let them win but unfortunately the events of 9/11 had created lots of fear in people, especially about flying.** All in all, the party went off without a hitch. It was one of the most uplifting events of my life to see Sarah so very happy. We all needed that after such a horrific tragedy.

But now I knew I had to get down to the nitty gritty and do all I could to make our show stand out of the hundreds of shows on the Strip.

Hotel employees were getting fired left and right. I made a conscious effort to never complain about having to go into work. I realized I was so blessed that I got to go in and do a job that I loved rather than having to show up at a job just to make money to pay my rent, bills, or medical insurance.

Companies downsized their staff, some more than half, so people had larger workloads and in many cases, their pay was also cut if they wanted to keep their jobs. I noticed the Riviera Hotel learned, like many companies, how to function with half the amount of employees than they had before 9/11. Less people in housekeeping, less dealers, less waitresses, less valets, less of everyone! **That was the first time I realized that anyone could lose everything they have in the blink of an eye.**

On top of all this going on, I was still worried about my voice. What if it were to get worse? I was, in fact, the most expensive part of the show and, at any time, could have been let go, but I had to just push forward and make myself indispensable. In fact, not one of the performers were fired from the show, but the people who took care of running the show were cut drastically. There were less ticket brokers (those are the people who work to sell tickets to guests). They were all working with skeleton crews. Many people definitely stepped up and multitasked, they would work on both seating and cleaning up but some people couldn't do both and that's what made the difference between who stayed and who was let go.

None of these TV appearances, radio interviews, etc... were required or part of my job but to keep me and the show going I knew I needed to be one of the multitaskers. I studied

Knowing I Had to Stay in the Spotlight

the things that were falling behind, and I focused on how I could boost them up, because I was desperate to keep doing what I loved.

I always felt like my producer had no idea what he was doing so it was all on me. It was a heavy burden on my shoulders. I spent half my time, in those 25 years that I did that show, trying to make my producer do something that was good for him. I had to step in front of him a hundred times in order to make him not trip over himself. Now that I am a producer, I realize that my instincts about him being a hack were absolutely right. **In hindsight, this was also where I learned that I could do the job of a producer, so I guess I could consider it a lesson.**

I was also doing it all for very selfish reasons in that I wanted to keep my job. Not only was I covering up my voice problem, but I was doing my producer's job while fending off the malice from the other performers who thought I was a publicity hound instead of seeing that I was desperately trying to drum up business for the show. Every commercial, television interview, and public appearance helped a little bit more to plug the show and it worked.

I was already resented by the cast for the fact that I had my own beautiful dressing room, personal wardrobe assistant, and the large salary I made for starring in the show. I was always smart in business and after four years of business college, I was not going to help somebody run their company, do all the work, and not get compensated for it. **I might have decided not to be a doctor, but I put my BA in Business to good use in show business.** People sometimes think I'm just a pretty face, but I think my 10 million dollar contract showed I was a lot more than that!

At times, my producer would pull in up to $100,000 a week for the show and you better believe I was going to get my

With Singer Rick Springfield Backstage After Headlining the 9/11 Benefit at the Mandalay Bay Stadium

portion of that. This money wasn't to cover show expenses. **It went straight into his pocket to build his ego** and every penny of it not only made him richer but made him seem more powerful. I was not going to allow that to happen and not get my fair share of it and my contract made sure of that. I basically got 20% of that for myself and the other performers hated me for it. I can't blame them but here's where the real talent came in. If you're smart enough to do your job in a way that makes you worth your salary, then you deserve it and I definitely deserved all I got.

I have a plaque at home that says, "Act your wage." I believe that money intensifies your personality, good or bad. If you're a bad person, money empowers you to do more bad things. If you're a good person it gives you the means to help other people. That is the difference between myself and my old producer. I didn't mention his name in this book because I don't ever want to give him notoriety again!

I've Done So Much With So Little For So Long That Now I Can Do Anything With Nothing

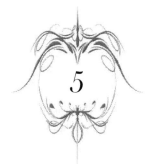

5

Good Investments Bad People

So between the scare of 9/11, the economic slump that occurred in Vegas, and since I still had my voice problems, I was always afraid that I could lose everything. I had the bright idea that if I invested my money and my voice never got better, I'd at least have something to fall back on.

Over the years I accumulated a substantial amount of money which I in turn invested with my stock broker, Larry. He went through three different brokerage firms while I was with him but he finally ended up at Merrill Lynch. I invested almost every penny I had with him, which I thought would be a safe and smart investment. Don't get me wrong when things were good, they were very good but apparently nothing good lasts forever.

Over our 10 year relationship, he made hundreds of thousands of dollars for me, but when the economy spiraled downward, he seemed more interested in the products that got him the highest commission rather than what would be

Frank Marino

The Best Investment I Ever Made Was in Myself

beneficial for me in my portfolio. **I felt like he put his financial interests before mine.** At one point he bought me a life insurance policy with a large premium payoff. Now that doesn't seem so bad, but if you think about it, I didn't have a spouse or any children and I had enough money to leave to the people I cared about. A life insurance policy is for people who don't have a lot of money but want to make sure that their children and their heirs are taken care of when they die. While the product didn't make sense for a single gay man with no children, it made perfect sense to him because that company gave him an abnormally large commission for selling it. As a stock broker, you advise your clients to invest in certain products. But on the flip side, a stock broker gets paid a kickback for selling certain products.

Larry didn't invest in the market trying to make me more money. Instead, he started selling me the products that gave him the most substantial kickbacks. After all, the economy had also affected him. He probably had a lot of people taking their money out of the market to pay their bills which caused him to earn fewer commissions. Unfortunately, I didn't know any of this at the time. **I had really trusted him.**

Nobody predicted the crash of the stock market. I can't tell you how frightened I was when I woke up and found the Dow Jones Industrial Average Index down over 500 points along with the NASDAQ and S&P as well. I called Larry almost every day out of fear and when it was a good day in the market he would answer the phone, and when it was bad, he would have me speak with his half-brother David, who was also a broker with the firm. Because of this, David and I grew to be good friends. It ended up being David who called me one day and told me, "My brother Larry really screwed you."

This one time Larry and David had a fight about my investments and he told me how Larry had only been selling me products that would give him the highest commissions. That was why Larry didn't want to talk to me directly anymore. Maybe he had a guilty conscience? Then David told me that I could file a lawsuit. I had no idea you could sue a financial institution. **I thought it was like gambling,** you take a chance and have to deal with the outcome. I found a lawyer, Alan Sacks, who specialized in stock fraud. He told me why and how all the things that Larry was doing were unethical, immoral and wrong.

It Was Much Easier to Cry in a Rolls-Royce

At one meeting where Larry did actually show up, he pulled up in his brand new Mercedes and I asked him, "How is everyone else losing money and you can pull up in a brand new Mercedes?" He just fed me back the same tired line. "All of my money is invested the same places as yours. It's just an up and down thing and you need to ride it out." After all, he was supposed to be the expert. I had trusted him, and therefore the betrayal made me furious! It reminded me of when my old producer bought a new mansion and I called it, "The house that Frank built." I'm always the work horse so other people like to live off of me. But this is not the first Hollywood story you'll hear like that and I'm sure it won't be the last!

I was very nervous. I was in no position to lose this large amount of money especially with my the voice problem and the economic crisis. Any day the curtain could come down. I had so much money invested. **There were times when I'd lose $20,000 to $30,000 in a single day.** I had given him my life's savings. I'm definitely the wrong person to be in the stock market when it's going through a volatile stage and acting like a roller coaster. I'm not going to lie, when things were good, I didn't complain, but when they got bad, they really got bad. What people don't realize is if you lose 50% of your portfolio in one year, even if you make 50% back the next year, you're still only at 75% of the original amount. In other words, if you lose 50% of $100,000 you have $50,000 left, but if you gain 50% back the following year on that same account, it's only 50% of $50,000 so that comes out to only $75,000. You're still down $25,000!

When I found out that you could sue a brokerage firm, I also discovered I had to sue all three brokerage firms that he was employed by while I was his client. What I wasn't prepared for was sitting at the arbitration table and them slinging accusations at me. I was the victim here. No one had ever spoken to me that way before.

It was very odd for me, but it was also my life's savings so I came right back at them. The lawsuit was for $650,000 and at the end of arbitration they offered me a settlement of around $300,000. My lawyers told me to say no. So I said no. I had never said no to that much money before. **To walk away from $300,000, I don't think I'd ever do that again under any circumstances,** but I had put my coat on and, in true movie star form, walked out the door — very much like Joan Collins who played Alexis from "Dynasty."

When we went to arbitration, their lawyer was the brother of Sharon Gless from the hit TV police drama "Cagney &

With Sharon Gless

With Joan Collins

Lacey." He came over to me on the break and said, "Listen, I have to be this way because I'm their lawyer, but I'm a big fan of yours." That helped settle my nerves.

Three days later, I got a call from the arbitrator and he said that he'd never lost an arbitration and he didn't want to lose one now. He wanted me to settle. **He gave me a settlement amount that wasn't exactly what I wanted but it was really close so I'd be a fool not to take it.** If it had gone to trial, there was a chance that **I could have lost everything, so I did the sensible thing and took it!**

Larry ended up losing his job and his brokerage license got suspended for a period of time. David and I stayed friends and we occassionally still talk to each other on the phone. I've since moved on to a trustworthy broker, Mike Chudd.

People Who Think Money Can't Buy Happiness, Just Don't Know Where to Shop

My Chérié Amour

In my quest of doing all my crazy appearances for publicity and willing to do anything to get on television, I did an interview for an article about a doggie psychic, who came to my house to do a cover story for *Dog Magazine*. She told me that my dogs, Maxine, a girl schnauzer, and Fluffy, a boy lhasa apsos, who had passed away, wanted me to get another dog, which I'd sworn I'd never do again, as not to have my heart broken the way it did for them. Coincidently, right after that, a TV show came to me called "Around Your Home." They offered to come and remodel a room in my house and surprise me with the results.

They toured my house and were stumped. My house was so perfect (and by perfect, I mean perfectly overdone – imagine Liberace on steroids), that they were in a fix for what to do. They said, **"Whatever we do, it's going to look simplified instead of an upgrade."** They then came up with the idea of redoing my dog run outside in my yard.

Frank Marino

The First Day with Cherié on Her Princess Bed

When I finally got to see the grand reveal, I was shocked. **They transformed my dog run and added a magnificent two-story doghouse complete with air conditioning and plush carpeting.** I had to hand it to them for coming up with something so unique and yet so perfectly my style. I'm very capable of doing my own decorating, but it was just so rewarding to have a talented decorator understand me well enough to give me exactly what I had wanted.

They also gave me the opportunity to go to a pet store and pick out a dog of my choice. I looked around and my heart actually skipped a beat when I saw the cutest little Maltese puppy I'd ever seen. She was just a little ball of white fur with the brightest, most playful eyes. Right then I knew. This was my next furbaby. I visited her every day until the taping was done. I doggy-proofed my whole house so that she'd be safe. **I named her Cherié after the french term mon cherié which means "my love."** Cherié was the perfect little bundle of joy that I needed in my life at that moment. I spent weeks filling her little wardrobe with designer dresses. She eats her dinner and drinks her water out of Versace dishes and gets carried around in a Louis Vuitton carrying case. Alex and I didn't have children, so Cherié became like a child to us. We love and spoil her as any parents would because she was our little princess.

From the first moment I held her in my arms, I felt responsible for this little life. I work nights so I got to spend all day with her. No matter what was going on in my life, she always loved me unconditionally.

Over the years she's been on so many television shows with me that top designers have even made

Cherié's Wardrobe Closet

duplicates of my gowns for her. I wouldn't leave the house without taking care of everything for her first. **Every day she gets her hair and teeth brushed by me.** She has a standing appointment at the groomer every Friday. She is the highlight of my day and the doggie love of my life.

For over 17 years this dog was nothing but amazing. She was trained right from day one. She never messed in the house. She went outside when she needed to, ate when she wanted and never ate too much since I always left food out for her. If I was having a bad day, she'd place her little paws on my arm and snuggle her head into my chest and just sat with me. I could never stay upset about anything when she was in my arms. I was always overwhelmed with joy when I was with her.

Alex, Cherié and I

Cherie and My Mother Sarah

Most of the time, we even let her sleep on a pillow between the two of us. At least three times a night, she would go and walk on Alex's head (she knew I needed my beauty sleep, so she didn't do it to me at all) so that he could take her off the bed and put her on the floor to use the dog run. She had this routine where she'd go outside to pee and then go in to get a drink of water, then comes back to the bed, where Alex, half-asleep, would reach down and put her back up on the bed. Of course, her habit of getting a drink after going out to pee made her need to pee an hour later again, so I don't think Alex had a full night's sleep in years.

When I Picked Her Up at the Hospital After Her First Operation

I learned a lesson early on with Cherié that you never train a dog. You, as the owner, get trained to make the dog do the correct things. In my opinion, Cherié has never done one thing wrong and that's why she was the only thing in my life that was zero headache. I never fed her people food; she didn't even know what it was and I think that's what kept her so healthy until recently.

At age 14, she was diagnosed with cancer. The veterinarian told us she had only three months or so to live, so at this point I hand-fed her anything she liked and three years later she was still a playful and happy little princess. I just thank God for miracles for without them, I wouldn't have had her for so long.

If you couldn't see the little cancer bump on her nose, you wouldn't have known that she was so sick or that she was 14 years old, which is 98 in human years. **She played all day and was always happy.** Once she got sick, she was still not a headache. The doctor said that she loved us so much that she

Cherié Resting in Her Mackenzie-Childs Doggie Bed

was fighting that much harder to stay around and be with us for as long as she could.

We actually ended up having three more amazing years with her, seventeen in total and until the end, she brought me joy every single one of those days.

No Matter What Went Wrong in My Life, Cherié Was Always My Mon Cherié

A Fortune in Free Facelifts

One fall day, my partner Alex said to me that he was thinking of going to the doctor to get some liposuction on his stomach. We went together for his pre-consultation and while we were sitting in the office with Dr. Anson, Las Vegas's number one plastic surgeon, I was telling her that I was thinking of getting my neck done the following year to make it a little sharper along my jawline. After Alex finished his consultation, he got his quote and we headed home.

An hour later, the phone rang, and it was Dr. Anson. She asked me if there was any chance that I'd be interested in getting my neck done this year, when I took my usual days off around the holiday season. I told her I was taking two weeks off for Christmas to take the family on vacation to Disney World, as I did every year. She then began telling me about this TV show called "Plastic Surgery: Before and After," and that if I was willing to do it just before my Christmas vacation, they'd love to have me on the show but also that they'd give the operation to me for free, my favorite word!

I immediately went through my schedule and told her that if we could do it on one specific date then I would have five days left to recuperate before our vacation. She fussed a bit about taking it easy after surgery, but after as much plastic surgery as I've already had over the years, she knew I'd know how exactly to take care of myself during recuperation, and I'd be fine.

At this point, since I only had this one day that would work, they said they'd get back to me. **All the stars must have aligned.** Dr. Anson, who is normally booked for months in advance, was miraculously free on that day and the producer for the TV show said they were open on that day as well. Now I was getting all excited — I could hardly believe how it all came together so perfectly. It, obviously, was meant to be!

Then, later that same day, I got another call that they really wanted it to be a human interest story. They wanted to know if there was anyone else in my family who would wanted plastic surgery. I immediately thought of my mother, Mary, so I called her right away. We were so much alike, especially when it came to the glitz and glamour. So I called her and said, **"You know, Ma,"** I told her cagily, **"not that you need it, but would you be interested in being on this plastic surgery show with me?"** She was a little hesitant about it. She'd never had any surgeries and on top of that to have it done on national TV made her very nervous. For me, this was old hat. I already had more than 10 plastic surgeries and three of them had been filmed for different television shows. I told her what she could expect and managed to talk her into it. **Secretly, I think, she really wanted it but just needed a little push.**

Then I got a call from Alex. He had mentioned the story to his mother, Malka and she really wanted to do it as well. This was around the time they had these TV shows like "The Swan," where people got those total transformation makeovers from top to bottom. She had watched them religiously and required no nudge. Well, they wanted a human interest story, so I called Dr. Anson and said, "Hey, I know you were going to do me and my mom, Mary, but what about putting my mother-in-law, Malka, into the mix?"

Once again, the stars perfectly aligned to do all three face lifts on camera. I went first and had my neck done then

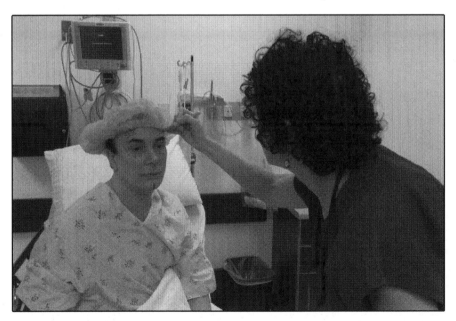

Dr. Anson Getting Me Ready for a Little Nip/Tuck

my mother, and my mother-in-law, who got full face lifts, neck lifts, forehead lifts, and nose jobs — all for free! **Between the three of us, we had over $100,000 worth of surgery, and poor Alex had to pay for his liposuction.**

The show was supposed to air only once that season, but it got such good ratings that they aired it three or four times that season and three more times every season for the next five seasons!

At this point, I was so used to getting plastic surgery that I knew what to expect. I know you look really bad before you look really good. I remember my mother calling me and

They've Done More Work on
My Face Than Mount Rushmore

Drags to Riche$

Malka, Me and Mary Recovering

Malka calling Alex, saying things like they didn't look the same. The person looking back in the mirror wasn't them anymore. I said, **"Were you happier kicking your chin down the street?"** In retrospect, I realize that I wasn't as consoling as they might have liked me to be. I think sometimes I wasn't born with the sympathy gene. Because of the difficult times that I've had to go through, it's often hard for me to relate to people whining about such small things. I try not to complain about life. I try to fix things and move forward and try to cope the best way I can. I learned through those hard times that sympathy can be a trap. It can sometimes make people wallow in pity instead of trying to find a solution. I think this is called "tough love."

There are times that I may seem cold to the people I work with, but when I ask a person who works for me to rearrange the furniture, I'm jumping right in there with them. **I never ask people to do anything that I wouldn't do myself.**

Besides, I knew that plastic surgery looked a lot worse than it actually feels but if you get caught up with the black and blue in the mirror, you can fall into that sympathy seeking mode.

The Big Reveal with Malka, Mary, Me, Sarah, and Alex After the Surgeries

In the end, once Mary's and Malka's swelling went down and their faces settled, they started getting lots of compliments. They found they really like the results and loved the new them!

The TV show followed us through each of our procedures and even afterwards where they wrapped up the episode with me getting my first star on the Las Vegas Strip. Receiving this star was not only the perfect conclusion for the plastic surgery show, but it brought local and national attention to the "La Cage" show at the Riviera. It was definitely a huge highlight of my career. **I was only the second person to ever get a star on the Las Vegas Strip after Mr. Las Vegas himself, Wayne Newton.** I got a lot of flack about this because, out of all the old-timers like Elvis Presley, Frank Sinatra, and Liberace, they couldn't believe I got mine first!

Mr. Las Vegas, Wayne Newton

When they held the big star unveiling ceremony, among the line-up of speakers were the Riviera Hotel President, Bob Vannucci, the entertainment columnist, Mike Paskevich from the *Las Vegas Review-Journal* newspaper, a spokesperson from the Walk Of Stars, and my show producer. **Although, as usual, out of sheer jealousy my producer refused to even show up for the ceremony, but then I didn't really want him there anyway.** Life has a funny way of working things out naturally.

Receiving My First Star

It's Hard to Do Extraordinary Things with Ordinary People

Success is Not for the Lazy

By now you know I would be willing to work 24 hours a day to make all my dreams come true. **Every single award or accolade that I've received is very special to me.** I don't take anything for granted, although sometimes I kind of feel the prejudice Sammy Davis Jr. must have felt with when he was asked to enter through back door of the hotel. I get invited to all the elaborate parties, red carpet events and show openings but it seems I always get invited last.

I think it's because I perform in drag, some people think it's a lower form of entertainment and that's because of their own ignorance. And I'm fine with that because, like Sammy, it has kept me laughing all the way to the bank for the past 35 years. **The fact that I keep jumping over the hurdles that they threw out at me and overcoming all the obstacles, I believe it's actually what gives me the drive to keep going.** I want to show other people that they can also do it too and to never take "no" for an answer.

It Takes a Lot of Work to Be the "Best"

Often, people who haven't seen my show are taken by their friends. I see them lined up outside my showroom. I can always spot the ones that are coming for the first time. They sometimes look a little unsure, like they've been "dragged" there (no pun intended). I actually love those people, because I also see them after the show and they're beaming with happiness and enthusiasm.

There's something about my show that changes the way people perceive what I do. I must be doing something right because not only is my show an unprecedented success, making me the longest running headliner on the Strip for over 35 years, but it always ends up making people happy. I'm often told that my show was the best part of their Vegas vacation. One of my favorite parts of the evening is when I get to greet my fans after every show. We get everything from prom kids to senior citizens and each one of them come out with a smile cheek to cheek. I'm not bragging, but I've spent

Drags to Riche$

My Home Office is Filled with my Accolades

about 35 years honing my craft and I do it really well. **The show's continued success proves that.**

    I have a belief that everyone is where they want to be in life. What I mean by that is that if you don't believe in yourself and you're continuously not getting ahead, then psychologically you might be holding yourself back. But if you believe in yourself and you think you deserve it, you watch how things come to you.

    My home office is filled with memories and accolades of all my accomplishments and I must admit, I do sometimes like to sit back and look at them. **Whatever your job is, if you get an award or trophy, put them up where you can see them every day.** I just look at the walls of my office and think about how lucky I am to be living out my dreams.

I received my first star on the Las Vegas Strip back on February 1st, 2005, when I was still working at "La Cage." It was placed in front of the Riviera Hotel and Casino.

I received my second star in front of the LINQ Hotel across from Caesars Palace on February 25th, 2010 for my 25th Anniversary as a performer on the Las Vegas Strip. I received the 45th star right after Dean Martin and Frank Sinatra. My first star was as a Las Vegas Headliner and my second was for being a Las Vegas Icon. It was recently moved to the front of the Paris Hotel.

The Las Vegas Walk of Stars has very strict guidelines for consideration. You can't just call up and buy a star. If it were that easy, I know lots of celebrities that would "buy" one. Actually, someone from the entertainment community has to submit your name. Then there is a board of a hundred people, most of whom are anonymous that go through the nominees and vote, but it has to be unanimous. Every single member of the board has to agree to vote you in.

Of the 70 different star recipients, I'm the only one to ever receive two of them.

Receiving My Second Star

Drags to Riche$

Celebration for My 25,000th Show

For my 25,000th performance on the Strip, I was presented with a key to the Strip and February 1st was declared Frank Marino Day. Then on my 20th anniversary as a Strip Headliner, the city council dedicated the street outside my house and named it Frank Marino Drive.

Street Dedication

The Frank Marino Slot Machine

The Riviera once made a $5 poker chip of me and the Tropicana made a $25 poker chip with my image on it, but I've moved up to my very own Wheel of Fortune table now in the LINQ casino pit and there is even a Frank Marino slot machine. **Now it's time for my Emmy and maybe an Oscar or two!**

I have to tell you, the one accolade I always wanted was my own wax figure. I had visited the Madame Tussauds

My Own Wheel of Fortune

Drags to Riche$

Receiving the Key to the City
From the Mayor, Oscar Goodman

Wax Museum here in Las Vegas many times and they have a room dedicated to just Vegas celebrities like Siegfried and Roy and others. When traveling the world, I found that the Madame Tussauds Wax Museum in New York City has a RuPaul wax figure. In London they have a Dame Edna statue as well. **It only made sense to me that the longest running headliner in Las Vegas should be included in their "Vegas" room.** So I had every one of my agents and managers go di-

Frank Marino

rectly to Madame Tussauds and ask if they'd consider me. Apparently, they only pick six personalities to make into new wax figures every year but year after year, I just never make the cut. Meanwhile, they have local magicians and a porn star, but not me. I just didn't understand it.

They have passed me over for 15 years now. I'm like the Susan Lucci of wax figures. One time they called and told me that if I paid for the statue, they would consider it. I had wanted it for so long, I agreed only to have them change their minds yet again. Another year, they told me that they were only doing interactive scenes, like George Clooney playing at the blackjack table so a person can go up and pretend they're playing blackjack with him for a picture. I had an answer for that. **I suggested that they could do a makeup vanity table and people could take a picture putting on their makeup next to me.**

Finally, this past year they came to me again and said they were trying to get the LGBTQ community's business, so if I wanted to contribute $100,000 for them to throw an LGBTQ party, they would finally make the wax figure of me, but by then I was over it. This time, I turned them down. **"My ego used to want to have this statue so badly but now I realize I don't have to have it,"** I told them. **"I do deserve it, so you should still do the statue of me."** But, the minute I wouldn't give them the $100,000, they wouldn't even consider it anymore.

You know I'm not one to let it go easily so I did call them and told them what they could do with their statue. The message was so foul that, needless to say, if I was the last person on earth they still wouldn't put me in their museum. I no longer have the desire to be part of their exhibit, but the good news is that last year I got something even better.

The Frankie Marino Doll

They came out with the Frankie Marino doll that ended up being so successful that I can now afford to buy my own damn wax figure **(if I wanted to)** from the doll profits alone!

I Am No Longer Accepting the Things I Cannot Change, I'm Changing the Things I Cannot Accept

9

The Last Day I Was Happy

April 25th, 2008 was my mother, Sarah's, 82nd birthday. About a month before that I had gotten a call from "The Maury Povich Show." They wanted to do an episode on people who had excessive plastic surgery. I then realized that the date of the show would land on my mother's birthday so I excitedly called my sisters back home on Long Island. I told them to tell her that they wanted to take her to "The Maury Povich Show" in New York City for her birthday but don't mention me being on the show. **I'll be a surprise guest and afterward we can take her to Central Park for dinner at Tavern on the Green to celebrate her special day.** Everything ended up working out like clockwork.

From backstage, I caught a quick glimpse of my mother's face when Maury announced me as his special guest star. She started to cry because due to my show schedule, I couldn't make it back home for many special occasions.

Frank Marino

Taking a Horse and Carriage Ride with Sarah, Alex, and Two of My Sisters Through Central Park

After the show, we had a great time treating my hometown like we were tourists. We took a double-decker bus tour all around Manhattan. **You know how it is when you live somewhere, you never go to see all the tourist attractions.** From the bus, you can see the Statue of Liberty, the Empire State Building and even Ground Zero where the Twin Towers used to be before 9/11. I'm glad we got the chance to see it all together like this.

After the tour, we went back to the hotel, where the Maury Show put me up, so we could freshen up for dinner. **I wanted my mom to look nice, so I took off her sunglasses to do her hair and makeup for dinner and I**

noticed that her eye was very red and irritated. I immediately got very worried and said to my sisters, "You have to take her back to the doctor, something's not right with that eye."

The team of opthamologists that she'd gone to had told her that it was just an allergy. She hadn't just gone once to these doctors. She'd gone several times and they kept telling her the same thing.

It took months of badgering the doctors for her to find out that she had a cancerous tumor, but by the time they finally realized there was nothing that they could do. We got the old line that if they'd caught it earlier, things would have been much different, **but unfortunately in our society when people are older, they seem to push them under the rug and pay them no attention.**

Enjoying Dinner at Tavern on the Green

Frank Marino

My mother finally got with an oncologist who diagnosed her with stage four cancer, and that began the six longest months of my entire life. I would call her 3-4 times a day so I could spend every available moment talking to her. I think my sisters got sick of me calling. I was so worried and I just wanted to hear my mother's voice. I knew that even with the treatments she was slowly deteriorating and starting to forget what was going on. I could hear it in her voice and my heart was breaking more and more with each call.

The night before my mom was permanently hospitalized, they called me up and said, "I think you should come home now." There was no question in my mind. I started packing and making arrangements to go home. One of those arrangements was to have Alex call my producer. I remember him saying, "You have to get a fill-in to do the show tomorrow night." I wasn't even thinking that he'd do anything but say okay. I couldn't imagine anyone cold enough to deny a person to be with their own mother on her deathbed. But his reply was, "This is show business and the show has to go on no matter what." I was floored. I didn't even think before I replied, **"Tell him, I don't care if he has to grab the damn microphone himself and shove it up his ass. I'm getting on a plane tonight and I'll see him when I get back.** I don't know when I'll be back but I had never taken off one day that wasn't pre-planned in 25 years. So I am taking this time to go be with my Mom." And I asked Alex to hang up. This discussion was over!

It ended up being the hardest two weeks of my life. Every day I would sit in the hospital room, holding her hand, or pacing while she laid there in a coma. There is a smell to cancer that no amount of flowers can mask. **I can actually smell the same scent on my dog Cherié ever since she has gotten sick. That smell is something you will never forget!** There was also the sound of call buttons, intercoms, and nurses shuffling from one room to another, a monotony that is broken only by the meals that she was too sick to eat, and more infrequent visits of the doctors who don't tell you anything helpful. I can still remember the feel of the sheets under my cheek where I used to lay my head next to hers as she slept. **I knew what it was going to feel like to lose a mother again.** My parents, the Marinos, had died years ago so I knew what my sisters were about to go through as well and I had to anticipate the arrival of the sadness that was inevitable.

Me and Sarah

Frank Marino

Sarah and Me at the Michael Bublé Concert

The echo of the grief for them haunted me on top of my grief for Sarah until the dread became real.

No matter how you try to prepare yourself, it doesn't matter. **The day she died, part of me died with her.** The funeral was a blur of people and sounds that felt as slurred as my speech. I know I slept very little, ate even less, and just witnessed the whole thing through the blur of tears. I stayed in town long enough for the funeral, but a piece of me never left that hospital.

When I came back to Las Vegas, I grieved really hard. For a while, my drive died with her. Alex would get phone calls from my friends saying, "What's happened to Frank? He's a shell of what he used to be." I did my job every night by

My Last Christmas with Sarah

going on stage and telling jokes but I was crying on the inside. I would go to all those functions that show biz requires of you, but I really just didn't want to be anywhere except in my bed. **Sleeping was the only thing that I wanted to do because when I was asleep, my mother was still alive.** There, in sleep, I found my only solace and I would sleep any time that I could. I fell asleep in nightclubs, at concerts, on

Sarah's Final Resting Place

cruise ships, at dinner parties. All I wanted to do was stay in that dream state so that I didn't have to deal with the fact that I no longer had, one of the people that I loved more than anything on earth. **I still needed her.** How could she be gone? I'd go to call her and instead I would call my sisters just to hear a familiar voice.

Since I was in show business, my mother was at many events with me. I had video tapes of different things we did together so I spent some time making a compilation video for my sisters for Christmas. Over that Christmas, my sister Nadine and I would watch it 2-3 times a day sobbing uncontrollably because I felt if I tortured and hurt myself enough, that I would push the pain out of me. As crazy as that sounds, that's what we did. My other siblings couldn't watch it at all. It was too much for them.

To this day, when I see someone who's grieving the loss of a family member, a parent, a child, I can feel my own grief resurface. Here is the primary place where I have empathy. There are, in life, few things that I can't grind through and this was one of them.

I spent almost three years where I faked it, sleepwalking through my life. I was just existing, not living. I really didn't care to live in a world without her by my side. Eventually, the pain does start to lessen and I realized Sarah would have wanted me to be happy and live life to the fullest, always remembering how special she was to me.

Grief is the Price You Pay for Love

The Producer From Hell

The year of my 20th Anniversary in "La Cage" should have been great for me, even with my voice problems. I had just finished filming the movie "Miss Congeniality 2" with Sandra Bullock. I was getting a lot of press coverage for the 20th Anniversary and I was on tons of television programs. **As a result, "La Cage" was really hot again!**

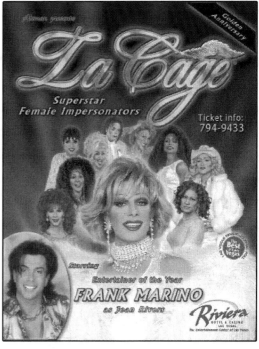

"La Cage" Program Book

You'd think my producer would have been grateful, maybe given me a gold watch or something for 20 years of service? Every interview I did was to promote his show. I wasn't required by my contract to court the press or promote "La Cage" at all, but **I did it because it made good business sense to me.**

So how do you think my producer showed his appreciation? Now we all know that there is no love lost between us but, in the middle of all this glory, my producer sent out a press release to all the media, saying that Frank Marino was not the only star in the show.

"Frank Marino is just one of the 15 performers. He's no more special than anyone else in the show."

Really? Yes, it takes a cast of 15 talented entertainers to make up the show, but no one can dispute the fact that for the past 20 years, I had been the star and face of "La Cage."

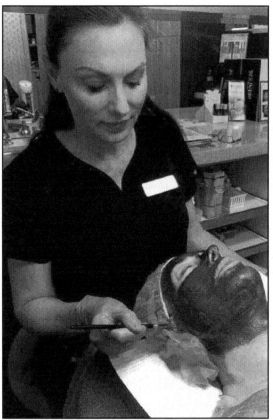

The Only Kind of Mud-Slinging I Like is a Mud Facial

After all the work I'd done to promote the show, he writes that garbage and sends it all over town. I found out about this when different magazines, TV shows and radio stations started to call me to ask what this letter they received was all about. I must admit that I was shocked. This was a new low, even for him.

I went to work that night and, very unlike my usual personality, I didn't say anything. I did my job just like every other night. I went onstage, told my jokes, introduced my fellow cast members and smiled. The audience laughed and had a great time as if it was just another show.

I was just waiting until my attorneys could contact him to let him know that I was aware of his slanderous press release. We sent a letter to him saying that I would like to

My La Cage Taxi Cab Advertising

be released from my contract or I was going to sue him for slander and defamation of character. Normally, these are two of the hardest things you can sue for unless the person sends out a press release to every single person in the media, which is exactly what he did!

So, here I was threatening a lawsuit and yet I still had to go to work every night and perform for this ungrateful person. But, if that weren't enough, the cast members were starting to be pitted against me. They were untruthfully told that the dispute was about my ego and that I wanted the show to be all about me when, in reality, I just wanted out.

That producer ended up pitting the entire cast against me. I remember one cast member getting crude. I'd been given a rhinestone bag by Judith Leiber to wear at my star presentation. I was excited and thankful. These are $10,000 purses, so in my speech I thanked the entire cast of the show just like I always did, but then I also thanked Judith Leiber and talked up the incredible purse. This cast member had the nerve to say that I'd spent more time thanking Judith Leiber for the handbag than I did thanking the cast for all that they'd done for the show. Of course, I had to come back with an even nastier comment. **"I'm sorry if you thought I spent more time on my new bag than you old bags."** I try never to start a fight but I definitely don't have a problem finishing one!

I often will use comedy to shield me from getting my feelings hurt. I'm always going to put a shiny finish of a joke onto something rather than dwell in the negative. I didn't let them see how much it hurt. These were my colleagues, some for over 20 years. We had spent every night together in the dress-

My Home Away From Home

ing rooms next to each other, passing one another backstage. It's very important to go on with a smile and introduce these acts in a way that gets the audience excited. **The audience should never know that anything is wrong backstage.**

But nothing could stop the nasty comments from some of the cast members who would constantly do many petty little things to try to annoy me for being the star of the show. Talk about a hostile work environment! Even my dressing room of 23 years was taken away from me and I was given an old storage closet. It was smaller than the washroom in my old dressing room. I felt like Shirley Temple in "The Little Princess."

I was at the lowest point of my career when it should have been the highest point. Instead of utilizing all that publicity, with me promoting the show my producer decided to try to put me in my place.

Luckily, my attorney was the number one power attorney, in this town for entertainment. We were in arbitration together for months. When it had all been hammered out legally, and my producer had finally agreed to the terms, I was extremely relieved. At that point, I just wanted to be able to do my own thing however on the day of the signing he refused to sign the agreement! He said, "I refuse to let you go. You'll have to sue me." I put my pen down on the table and walked out of the conference room. **The arbitration hearing had just been another trick to get me to stay longer. He just wanted to taunt me. What wouldn't this man do?**

I paced back and forth in my attorney's office. I was ready to fight. I remember the click of my attorney's pen on the desk as he told me, "You will win, but you've only got a year and a half left on your contract. Just stick it out and then you can go and do your own thing, because the case could go longer than that and will cost you thousands and thousands of dollars to fight it." The wind went out of me. My stomach got a little sick at the thought of another year and a half of working my ass off for that ingrate but what else could I do? **My attorney told me to go to work and take my check. Why waste thousands suing him?**

I continued to work, but I would be damned if I'd still do all the extras. It was harder than I'd thought it would be to stop doing all the publicity that I'd been building up for so long. You'd think I'd just sit back and enjoy the ride, but sitting on my hands was harder than actually doing the work. It's just not in my character so, **I did what I had to do which was performing on stage.** I didn't do any of the magazine articles, radio spots or television shows and I began to see the destruction of the "La Cage" empire that I had helped build over all these years start to crumble right before my very eyes. I just knew this was going to be a very difficult 18 months, or would it be?

He Finally Ended Up Cooking the Goose that Laid the Golden Egg

11

The Death of "La Cage"

I'll never forget the date — February 9th, 2009. I thought I had 10 months left on my contract, but instead, it was the day we got the news "La Cage" was closing. I remember that night vividly. We had just finished what I thought was an amazing show. There was a bit of a scuffle backstage between the cast members. I could hear faint sounds of private conversations. Then our producer walked in and announced that the show we just finished would be our last. **After 25 years, the show was over in a flash.** This would be the last time I ever saw or heard from this man again. Twenty-five years of him controlling me ended with a nod of his head and a brief wave. Want to talk about bittersweet. I'd dreamt of this day for many years, to finally be out from under his reign, but this was also the first time in a quarter of a century, I didn't have a job.

The "La Cage" Cast

I felt sorry for some of the other cast members. They were shocked, so I'm sure they would look out every night and see very large crowds thinking the show was doing great, but what they didn't see were the numbers that I was seeing. They didn't know that, since I stopped promoting the show, half of those seats or more were seat fillers (free tickets given out as comps from the casino floor).

We had survived four presidents, three wars, the turn of the century, and 9/11. But when the bumps came this time, without my help with the sales and public relations, the show ended up closing. I must admit I did feel a bit vindicated knowing that I was, after all, the driving force that made that show so successful, sort of like when Diana Ross left the Supremes.

It had been hard to watch the numbers fall those last few months. Even though some of the cast had turned on me, I still had a few friends there. I was letting the show fail on purpose. I'd been told to lay off the publicity, so I did! Besides this, I had enough on my plate with my mom's death and my voice problems.

Some of the cast had tried to get press but they couldn't do what I did. So the show's exposure went down tremendously. The show just didn't have enough juice any-

Two of the Biggest Divas Diana Ross and Me

more to take that last hit. I knew the producer couldn't run the show on his own. He hadn't realized, appreciated, or ever acknowledged, even to himself, how much I was taking care of things behind the scenes. I knew that no one was keeping relationships up with the ticket agents and brokers. I knew that without me doing the work, the show would eventually stop. Although, I didn't expect it to fall apart so quickly.

The day after the show closed, I remember I was scheduled to go on the morning news, doing a favor for a friend and talking about a special nail polish for Valentine's Day that he was using in his hair salon — a little fluff piece for fun. **While getting ready that morning, all of a sudden I looked** up and I was actually the lead story on the program about Las Vegas' longest running headliner closing at the Riviera Hotel. At that point the calls started pouring in from all the other television stations. I ended up packing five different outfits in the trunk of my car so that I could change my look for each one of them. **And there I was once again, a PR machine back in the swing of things doing what I do best only this time I was doing it for myself personally, not for the show.**

As the days went on, it started to become very surreal to me. I couldn't believe it had really happened. Even having known that it was coming, this had been my life for almost 25 years. I had been hired at the Riviera for a three month gig that last a quarter of a century. It also had transformed me into a Las Vegas Icon. Being the star of "La Cage" was all I knew, it had become my identity.

After the show closed, people would ask me what I did for a living. I didn't know what to say. I mean, if someone asked Paris Hilton what she did for a living, she'd probably be stuck for an answer too. She's Paris Hilton. That's what she does. I'm Frank Marino. That's what I do. Nowadays when people ask, I just reply I'm the "Queen of the Las Vegas Strip."

Actually, there was one point when I started feeling very sorry for myself, which is a very dangerous place to be. I had lost my Mom who was the most precious person in the world to me. I'd been released from the job, which defined me. And then there was my voice troubles making it so that I couldn't even express myself and how I felt about it all. What was I to do now? I wanted to call my Mom. I wanted her to tell me that

Drags to Riche$

Leaving My Dressing Room at the Riviera When "La Cage" Closed

I would bounce back. I wanted her to tell me that my voice would get better, and that someone would pick up the show.

(In reality, I didn't have to work anymore. I could coast. I could spend the rest of my life lounging by the pool. I was lucky enough to have saved enough money to live very comfortably for the rest of my life.)

I knew that there were other people who had it much worse than me, but when you're in the bleakest moments in your life, you just don't think about that. When you're in that dark place, you can only think of yourself. I had to break out of that. **I felt my mother's spirit kick me out of that dark place and back into life.**

"Tony and Tina's Wedding"

That's when I knew I had to get my name back on a Strip marquee. Vegas is a very fickle town. They'll forget who you are in six months. Lucky enough, I was immediately cast into the Vegas production of the off-Broadway show "Tony and Tina's Wedding" as a special guest star, doing a part they wrote especially for me. I was playing Frank Marino, a famous drag queen, who was also an ordained minister and married Tony and Tina. It was during that show, I noticed how much the audience still loved me. I thought, "What am I doing?" **These people love me. I was meant to be on stage.** I couldn't give this up and let them down.

With my mother's spirit in my heart and the fans applause in my mind, I turned myself around. It was only then that I finally started to think of my mother's death every other minute of the day instead of every minute. It took the death of my career at "La Cage" to help me start to overcome the death of my mother. Life is funny that way.

Keep Your Heels, Head and Standards High!

12

I Wasn't Done Talking

While I was performing in "Tony and Tina's Wedding," I experienced a really bad night with my voice. By the time I got home to Alex, I was a mess. **I asked Alex to research blogs on Dysphonia on the internet.**

Dysphonia is a muscle problem involving the tongue. It makes the nerves misfire when you're trying to talk and you end up slurring your words. In a little post that was really more of a side-blurb, we found our little ray of hope. It stated that there is a rare side effect from taking Paxil. Only one in a million people get it, but it causes Dysphonia. (I can't win the lottery, but I can win that.) A million in one chance... and I get it!

Once we found the first site mentioning it, we found others. People were begging for help in these chat rooms. It was heartbreaking. At last, I wasn't alone. But these were mostly complaints, and stories of the same type of misdiagnosis from doctors that I had experienced. Some complained

Frank Marino

Alex and I Posing for the No H8 Campaign

that they couldn't speak, others that they couldn't swallow, but all crying out for a cure.

We searched and read everything until our eyes felt like they were bleeding but finally we found websites where a few people mentioned a cocktail of three drugs, that if taken together had helped them to be able to speak again. One was lorazepram which is used to calm you down and one was trihexyphenidyl, muscle relaxer. I don't remember the third one because I never took it past the first week.

I ran to call the doctor. I didn't care that it was 2 am. If there was the slightest chance that I could get my voice back, I wanted to try it. I had to beg my doctor to please, please just try it but he said no. My regular doctor wasn't willing to prescribe something based on a chat room diagnosis without research behind it. I had to admit I saw his point, but I was desperate for a cure.

I went to two or three other doctors but they also said that they wouldn't do it. It wasn't until I went to one of my yearly touch-up sessions with Dr. Anson, my plastic surgeon, that I mentioned these drugs and my frustration to her. She called around to some specialists that finally led me to Dr. Glyman. He specialized in facial reconstruction that had to do with the jaw and speech.   He said, "Well, you've tried everything else, let's give this a shot." He was definitely a life saver.

It didn't happen overnight, but I did feel it was working, gradually. Every day, I started slurring a little less until one day it was 100% perfect. **To me, it was like a miracle that had happened. After 10 years of torture, this was all over!** It was sort of like a blind person regaining their eyesight and getting to see the world in a whole new light again.

I'm Like a Seed, Bury Me and I'll Grow Even Stronger

13

The Birth of "Divas!" One Rhinestone at a Time

Around the time I started getting my voice back, Alex was working as the Vice President of SPI Entertainment, a Las Vegas production company. He had worked his way up the corporate ladder. SPI Entertainment is involved with many Las Vegas shows on the Strip. I told him, "Why don't you quit and come with me. We'll do the show together. **You do the business and I'll do the show."**

Alex told me that his boss didn't want him to leave as he was much too valuable so he asked if I'd be interested in coming over to SPI. The idea was that he could still work on the Divas show with me and also keep working on their shows, making everyone happy.

I wasn't sure at first. **I told Adam that I would want full control.** I never want anyone to tell me that the dress should be red instead of blue. After working for a madman for

With My Partner Adam and His Wife Bri

almost 25 years, I didn't want to get caught up in that kind of power struggle again.

Adam totally understood my concerns and we came to terms. **I got my creative control and final decision on all things related to "Divas."** Adam and I went into business together creating a limited liability company called Her-Larious Entertainment of which I'm 70% and he's 30%. However, with this behind us, the next step was to go out and sell the show to a casino. I had no idea how hard the struggle to secure a showroom was about to be.

I had so many doors slammed in my face that I didn't need to have all those nose jobs. It appeared nobody wanted to put me in their theater.

The entertainment directors had every excuse in the world how to tell me that their customer was not really my audience. In turn, they didn't want **a gay show** in their casinos, but what is a gay show? Did they think that only gay men would want to see a show that involved a bunch of female impersonators? Yeah, because movies like "Mrs. Doubtfire," "Tootsie," "Priscilla Queen of the Desert," and "To Wong

Wearing High Heels to Climb the Ladder of Success

Foo" had such limited audiences, right? They didn't realize that with "La Cage" having been at the Riviera for almost 25 years, there must be a market that it was fulfilling. And let's not forget the celebrity impersonation part. **After all, I am the world's most famous Joan Rivers impersonator!**

My audience is middle America. I've seen and met my audiences after every show for 25 years. I knew who came to see my show. Sure, I bring in gay people, but the majority of my audience are couples and families from all over the country. If you've seen the show, you get it. If you haven't seen the show, what's wrong with you? Go see it!!

When I began building "Frank Marino's Divas," I took all the elements that I knew had worked from the old show, and I got rid of the things I didn't think worked. For instance, in "La Cage" we had a Michael Jackson impersonator, and although he was great, I didn't feel a male celebrity belonged in a drag show. I knew the winning formula and I knew I could make it work.

Me with Superstar Cher

That's why we keep all the fan favorites like Cher, Madonna, Diana Ross, and yet we throw in Rhianna, Katy Perry and Britney Spears for the younger crowd. There is a little something for everybody. We appeal to both sexes. I have the fashion for the ladies and my jokes are risqué enough for the men.

Hanging with Britney Spears

I remember meeting the one-time President of the Imperial Palace Hotel, Don Marandino at the opening party for another show. Marandino said that he'd be interested in putting my show in their late-night show slot at the Imperial Palace Hotel. I was so excited so we set up a meeting to discuss the idea.

But, as usual, when I came into that meeting, everybody

Black-Jack Anyone

Uncle Sam-antha · Labor Day 2009

kidding around at the board table, except Don, said they didn't think it was a good idea. They were talking about me like I wasn't even there. I took it and took it and then I finally snapped. And when they do the movie of my life story, it's going to be just like Joan Crawford in "Mommy Dearest" yelling at the executives from Pepsi Cola telling them, "Look fellas, this isn't my first trip to the rodeo." So I said, "Ok, how about you give me a one-night show Labor Day weekend and if I do well you keep me and if I don't do well, I'll go home." **Marandino says, "Deal," and as I looked at everyone around the table I could tell they were pissed.**

I didn't care. It was a foot in the door. I called and started gathering up my cast. People I knew were the best in the business, people my ex-producer thought were too expensive to hire. I called in all my favors to set designers, lighting techs, sound engineers, etc. and pulled everything in a short amount of time and we put on a fabulous show Labor Day Weekend. **I tried to use everybody I could from the old show that made sense.** Even with my ex-producer calling Caesars Entertainment and making up lies about owning the footage I was using on the electronic marquees to try to shut us down but the showroom was still packed and we were an immediate hit. We surpassed everyone's expectations.

When the executives saw the show and how jazzed everyone was, they asked us if we'd like to join

Auditioning the Frank Marino Dancers

Frank Marino

It Wasn't Going to Be Our Last Supper After All

the Caesars Entertainment family. I was ecstatic! I thought, okay, we'll start the show up in the high season, which is early February, but that wasn't what they offered.

"No, if you want the deal, you have to open the show now. You have five weeks and we want you to open in October."

This was Caesars Entertainment. They're the largest casino entertainment company in the world. When Caesars Entertainment says they want you in five weeks, you don't say, "Can you wait?" You say, "Okay!"

So I got the gig at the Imperial Palace, which has since been renamed the LINQ Hotel and I'm now the longest running headliner at the newest hotel on the Strip.

Alex has since become the Senior Vice President and COO of SPI Entertainment, but he also likes to do some creative stuff as well, like lighting and helping with the props, having the sets built, and picking the music, etc. I work on costumes, wigs, choreography and, of course, my specialty, the PR. **We make the perfect team.**

There are all these little things that people don't think about when they see the show. The entire set had to be configured so that it could be folded down and packed away in a tiny space about the size of a rubic's cube so they could be built up or taken down in 20 minutes since most showrooms are shared by multiple shows. The stage and lighting had to be scheduled during these miniscule time slots around other shows that already had dibs on the stage area. Due to the limited pre-production time, the show had to be based on raw talent more than the sparkle and glitter of the props, sets and lighting.

Me with the Frank Marino Dancers

Frank Marino's "Divas" had to be amazing. You'd think, with all the pressures of having to put together my new show that I'd be stressed, and I was, but it wasn't the same kind of stress. It wasn't the negative stress of being kept down, but more of a fulfilling kind of stress. The stress of wanting to do the best job for myself. Don't get me wrong, I loved the work. I had 25 years of ideas that I couldn't wait to put into action. It was my best work ever, but it was a 24 hours a day job. I don't think I would have minded if it hadn't been so hard on my relationship with Alex.

I didn't want "Divas" to be "La Cage." I wanted it to be so much more. "La Cage" was a cabaret show and I wanted "Divas" to be a large production show, a cross between "Chippendales" with hot male dancers and the old "La Cage" show with the world's best celebrity female impersonators.

To make matters even more complicated, in the middle of us trying to put "Divas" together there were some upheavals

"Divas" Billboard

The "Divas" Tour Bus

in the management of the hotel. First we lost Don Marandino right after Labor Day, but luckily, I'd won over the rest of the board by then. The remaining board members dropped like flies after that to be replaced by new people who had to be convinced once again that my show was the right fit for their hotel.

As **"Frank Marino's Divas" became a regular show at the LINQ, Alex and I were working together day and night to make changes to make it a success!** It took so much more work than I thought it would. Where I used to do the promos for the old show with the ticket sellers and so forth, I now had to do it on a much bigger level. **Once it seemed like it was going to calm down and I**

"Divas" at Work

could focus on maybe changing my act some, Caesars Entertainment decided not to renew the lease on the name Imperial Palace and changed the hotel name to The Quad.

I'd just gone through rebranding all my advertising from the Riviera to the Imperial Palace. Now I had to change it all again. We're talking billboards, cab toppers, cups, magazine ads, thousands of coupons. It cost me upwards of a hundred thousand dollars to redo it all. Alex and I scrambled to get it all done, and it seemed to us that no sooner had they changed to the Quad, they changed it again to the LINQ Hotel and Casino and we had to do it all over again!

Now the concept with the LINQ was for a minimalistic design so we lost all our in house advertising. No more casino floor posters, no more brochures at the check in desk, no more in room table tents or television ads. No more signs on the casino floor and worst of all, my face was taken off the front of the building which was our biggest piece of Strip advertising.

To add insult to injury, as they were remodelling the hotel, my dressing room was right in the path of construction. The new hotel was going to have cathedral ceilings on the casino floor. The new ceilings impeded my dressing room by two feet, which meant that I had to evacuate during construction. **They made me move to a hotel room, but not just any hotel room. The room they gave me was on the other side of the building.**

"Divas" Larger Than Life

My Beautiful Dressing Room

My dressing room has over 50 wigs, thousands of gowns, and lots and lots of make-up. Everything is perfectly organized and in its place like an operating room. **All my**

tools are laid out within reach. When I go make myself up, it's a precise procedure and when I reach for something by memory, it needs to be right there.

So now, during all this construction, my new dressing room was so far from the theater, it was about a 10 minute cab ride and that was only if we were able to make all the lights. LOL! I was exhausted! I changed outfits over 17 times a night. You do the math. Nobody had any idea of what I had to go through physically to put that show on every single night during that construction period. The good news was that it was such a workout that I think I lost a few pounds without even trying.

"Divas" was able to jump every hurdle even though we were wearing high heels. So much so that we ended up with two shows. We now have the resident show at the LINQ but we also have the traveling show that often plays Reno, Laughlin, Atlantic City, Connecticut, California, Indiana, and practically anywhere in the US. **I made it happen through sheer force of will. This time it was all mine and I wasn't going to let anything stop me.**

Never Quit Your Daydreams

14

The 20 Year Itch

I believe that working those kind of hours with that intensity is what makes a person a Diva. I know that, like any other Diva, when things don't go right, I can throw a tantrum. It's not like I ever asked someone to do something I wouldn't have done myself, but I expected it to be done at least up to my standards, the way I would have done it if I had done it myself. When they didn't, it just makes me crazy and I've been known to lose it.

Alex and I at the Wynn

Although my anger was never directed at Alex. When I ask him for help on something, he knows exactly what I like. He and I never had that kind of friction.

However if you've ever watched someone you love losing their temper constantly, it takes you back a step. I think that's what happened to Alex. He felt like he had to step in and smooth things over or calm me down, and he started to not like what he saw in me with all that anger.

He would always play good cop to my bad cop. Alex would rather have everyone compromise and be copacetic all the time.

To add to the problems, even with the time we spent together, 100% of that time was spent talking about work. **You don't put a show like "Divas" together in five weeks**

Alex and I on a Skiing Trip

Alex and I at My Brother Alan's Wedding

without devoting yourself to it 200%! We would go out to eat and end up talking about contracts. We'd be out with friends and the conversation would turn to set design, or someone's act, or someone's costume. When I was working, I was always working and when I wasn't working, I was chomping at the bit to get back to work or to finish just one more thing — not to mention that Alex had his full-time job at SPI with five other shows to worry about.

So it became pretty bad. **With the stress of doing the jobs of 25 people between us, the lack of attention to our relationship, and the unending task load of the new show, we ended up almost letting the relationship die.**

New Year's Eve 2013, Alex and I went out to dinner with friends and then on to a party at my partner and his boss Adam's house. See, even New Year's Eve turned into a work event. I thought we had a good time at the party but when we got home Alex was looking at photos in my phone from earlier that evening and stumbled across a few that were recently taken.

Alex and I at the New Year's Dinner

He felt that in those pictures, I looked so much happier with other people than I did with him. I didn't know what to say.

He said, "I think we should break up, because obviously we're not good together in a relationship anymore. It's turned into more of a business relationship than a personal one."

I thought he was crazy. I thought we were great together. Sure, work had been intense, but I still loved him. He had to know that. I wanted to make it work, but I looked in his eyes and I just knew that he'd already made up his mind.

When you're in a relationship, you realize that you're 50% of that relationship, but when your part-

ner wants to break up, they have 100% of the control. I ended up not having a say in it at all.

Still, I didn't see it coming. Maybe I should have? I was just so busy and I didn't give our relationship enough attention. We were so exhausted from working day in and day out. I think we loved each other, but right now we didn't really like each other anymore.

We still had to work together and we agreed to also keep living together. **I would hope to myself that it would be okay and we'd work it out eventually.**

Around the same time, I was a big fan of the TV show "Millionaire Matchmaker" and I watched every episode of it. **One of the casting directors, Marcy who now has since become a very good friend of mine contacted me on Facebook and asked if I was interested in being a guest.** I just thought it was very strange that I had just broken up with Alex and all of a sudden I'm being asked to go on this dating show. **If I've learned anything in my life, it's that everything happens for a reason.**

In order to qualify to be on the show, they do an extensive background check including a psychological evaluation to make sure you're not crazy and bank statements to make sure you really are a millionaire. I swear I've bought homes that required less paperwork. Of course, I passed with flying colors!

I remembered from watching the show how Patti Stanger could be tough sometimes so I was a little nervous, but when it all came together and I got to meet Patti she was wonderful. We got along right off the bat because she had done her college

Filming "Millionaire Matchmaker"

thesis on a friend of mine who was also a female impersonator in Florida that I met when I first started. Unfortunately, he has since passed away.

To try and impress her, I had dressed up in drag to look like Patti and had taken a photo to give her as a gift to break the ice. She got a real kick out of it. Patti must be a little psychic. She saw right through me just like she does everyone. When she asked me about my previous relationships, I didn't want to bring up Alex, but I think she sensed the deep pain I was trying so hard to hide. **When she asked if I thought Alex was my soul mate, I had to answer truthfully and said, "Yes, I do."**

Patti proceeded to give me some really good advice, both on and off camera. **She advised me to try to not be the star and deflect questions back to the potential dates rather than start some kind of fawning session over myself.**

I must admit, I had a really great experience on the show plus I got to meet a lot of really nice people. At one point, one of the producers whispered in Patti's ear to ask about my various plastic surgeries and she snapped back saying, "I'm not going to ask him about his plastic surgery."

I just smiled and said, "It's okay. Go ahead and ask me." I've done so many TV shows and interviews about all my plastic surgeries that it doesn't bother me to talk about them." To me, it's not a dirty little secret like it is to most celebrities.

Right before the mixer when we're supposed to meet all these potential suitors, I was introduced to the other millionaire that they had on my episode, and I was thinking, "Wow, we need look no further." **Here was exactly the type of guy I was looking for. He was cute, and was really well dressed.** The only problem was that he was straight.

For those that don't know, the format of the show is that first Patti coaches you a little bit as an introduction. Then you meet the other millionaire and the two of you go to this cocktail mixer where you get to meet a bunch of potential dates. You pick two of those people for mini-dates where you get to talk for a few minutes alone to get a feel for them, and then you pick a final date where you take that person out somewhere.

During the cocktail party, I was trying to remember Patti's advice and deflect the questions asked

Patti Stanger and Me

about me back to them. However, sometimes out of the corner of my eye, I was watching that other millionaire talk to his potential ladies he could choose from. The guys Patti had picked out for me were nice enough, but no one was standing out as a front runner for my potential final date.

I was thinking, I don't want to date just anyone. I want to date somebody equally successful. I wanted to be the guy in the back seat, not driving for once. I thought to myself what a nice guy this other millionaire was, so I finally got up my nerve and I asked Patti to bring him over. I joked, "Do you think there's any chance you'd ever consider dumping the bitch and making the switch?"

I was very cordially turned down, but we've become good friends since then. Patti coached me through the mini-date selection, and I think I more or less flipped a coin at that point. I'd already come this far and the cameras were rolling.

Needless to say, I flew my final date from Los Angeles to Las Vegas, and our first stop was zip-lining down Fremont Street. I was definitely pushing one of my fears with the zip-lining thing.

Honestly, I probably wouldn't have gone on the zip-line if the cameras weren't recording. **To make it worse, in order to get the camera angles they needed, they made us do it twice!!**

Unfortunately the date got worse from there. All he wanted to do was drink and I'm not a drinker myself. In any case, I haven't seen him since and I still have people express sympathy for me about that poor guy who ended up looking like a drunk on national TV.

At the beginning of the show, Patti had hit it on the head with Alex. I had already found my soul mate.

Ironically, this heartache is probably one of the best things that's ever happened to me careerwise. It brought me national exposure and lots of new fans. The public loved it so much that it's years later and they still rerun that episode.

I didn't realize the power that Bravo TV would have with my target audience. It was the first time that I'd really appeared as myself, not in drag. There were, however, clips of me in drag from my show on that episode, but for the most part, the show wasn't about the Divas show. It was about me, Frank Marino, the person.

Because people finally got to see the real me out of drag, I was being recognized more often. We were in Hawaii in a surf shop. I was wearing my little beanie cap that makes me look like a gangster and

Trying to Be Incognito

a woman came up to me and said how she saw and loved me on "Millionaire Matchmaker." It is a great feeling to be recognized wherever I went now.

All this new success was great but success is nothing without someone you love to share it with. Since Alex and I were still not together, I tried to date other people.

One of the guys I had dated after the "Millionaire Matchmaker" was Shawn. He lived in Las Vegas, New Mexico. He and I tried to make a long-distance relationship work. That didn't really pan out but we became great friends. He actually moved out to Las Vegas, Nevada with his new boyfriend and he now works for me. Shawn actually looks like a younger version of Alex and it was a little awkward at first, but eventually all three of us became friends.

Shawn and I

Frank Marino

Another Hard Day's Work with Shawn

During the six months we were broken up, I would tell Alex, "This is ridiculous. We should just get back together."

The whole thing came to a head when he went out with someone else and it really broke my heart. He'd made plans to go out of town with some guy that he'd been chatting with. I watched as he packed his suitcase. I realized I couldn't go on like this anymore.

When he came back, I asked him, "Is this how you want it to be? Because if it is, then it's about time that we truly split and go our separate ways."

It wasn't an ultimatum. I wasn't angrily challenging him, I was honestly professing my love for him. I was asking him to not end the relationship. I went on and on about our history. It felt like we had this conversation a million times before but this time, I wasn't giving up. I couldn't. He was the one and all this dating other people had just shown me there wasn't another Alex. We talked through the night and into the next day.

It turned out that his little vacation had been a wake-up call for him as well. Maybe he'd been expecting something different. He hadn't wanted to tell me before because he hadn't wanted to get my hopes up about getting back together, but his dates hadn't been any more meaningful than mine.

After that we did finally back together, we had the most amazing rekindling of our relationship. It was very romantic. Our relationship is now stronger than ever. Finally, we took the time to just be with each other and after six months of being broken up, we learned how important

Alex and I In San Francisco

it was to break away from the business long enough to enjoy one another.

I love him now even more than I did the first years we were together. I was on top of the world. The pieces of my life were all back in place where they belonged. The show was doing great, my voice was perfect, and now Alex and I were back together stronger than ever.

But life had one more big surprise in store for me and by now you know that I'm not good with surprises. Anyone who knows me, knows that I like to plan things out to the smallest detail before doing them.

One special night, I was ending the Divas show with my usual bit. I parted the curtains, I took my bow, two gorgeous dancers in tuxes offered me their hands and I walked down the stairs for the final bow. **My first clue that something was different was when the music kind of skipped, and you can see from the look on my face in the YouTube video that I was thinking, "Somebody's going to get it!"**

I thought something was going really wrong. All of a sudden Alex's voice came from the side of the stage and I was totally confused. Now since it was Alex, I began to calm down. I mean I trust Alex. He introduced himself and then on the

Love Is In the Air

Ipads and phones in the audience there were videos of people I know and love Skyping into the show. Still, I was just shocked enough to not know what was going on.

Contrary to what everyone later thought, I had no idea what he was up to. Everyone thought that we did it for publicity but I had truly no idea. I was watching the video on the side screen and I finally got it. Alex was doing a tribute for our 20th Anniversary together.

I was touched by the video. We'd been through so much together. He had put all these pictures from our life together up there. Pictures of family, vacations, our dogs, our milestones together both professionally and personally.

Here I was, getting all teary-eyed over the video and as it ended I turned around and there he was on one knee. I

Alex Proposing to Me Live On-Stage

swear I almost joined him down there but there was no way to get back up gracefully when you're wearing high heels and a Versace gown!

I saw the box. But it still didn't register. I saw the ring, but I turned away, overcome with emotion. I turned back and pulled him up and kissed him. My throat was closed up but I managed to choke out a heartfelt, "Yes."

"Is that a yes?" he asked.

There's only one way that I deal with that amount of emotion, happy or sad or bitter. I crack a joke.

"Does that mean you get 50%?" I quipped.

Alex was ready for me though and this shows how well matched we are. He didn't miss a beat when he said, "No, I get 70%!" "That's my man," I thought.

"Yes, I'll marry you," was the only answer after that.

I'm Very Easy-Going, as Long as Everything is Going My Way

15

With Great Love Comes Great Loss

At this point everything seemed to be going well, Alex and I were back on track and stronger than ever. I was finally starring in my own show, "Frank Marino's Divas Las Vegas" and my voice was now completely back to normal. We had sold-out crowds and magnificent reviews. That was where I was in life when Joan's death blindsided me, but that was only to be the first of many deaths to come.

One of the best things that happened a few years before was that my birth mother, Mary, relocated to Vegas and bought a condo around the corner from me. She came here with her husband, Lou, to retire but it was more than that which drew her to Las Vegas. Like me, Mary loved being in the spotlight and my celebrity and notoriety allowed her to be the center of attention as we traveled the world and attended amazing parties and events.

Mary Pitched in Everywhere

Mary and I got along so well, that it only made sense to ask her to work with me. I mean, she came down to the show every night anyway. She didn't have to work. She did it out of love and that made all the difference. She became the Divas brand ambassador and stage mother to all the impersonators and dancers. To this day, I still get people asking me about her. If you've been to the show, you've probably met her as well. **I spend most of my day at the theater, so having Mary right there was very comforting to me. We loved working together.**

As busy as I was, I would sometimes just stop and watch her work. When I would enter a room where she was, I would relax a little. I could literally see that I got so many traits from her but they were different from the traits I got from my upbringing with Sarah. Certain traits you are born with and certain ones you are taught. Working together 24 hours a day and having a ball, we got to see just how alike we were. I didn't see her for the first 28 years of my life and yet, some of the strongest traits I have were just like hers.

Mary never complained. Like me, she'd rather work through physical discomfort than bother those around her with it, but I could see that she was having trouble with her knee and hip. These joints had been giving her some trouble for months before she went to the doctor. She had put it off, thinking that it was just her age but after finally seeing a doctor, he told her that she had a tumor in her hip that she needed to have removed, immediately!

Alex Had to Deal With Two Divas

Here she was working with me during the day selling tickets, and at night selling merchandise and pitching in anywhere she could. **She was doing an amazing job, of course, after all she was my mother!** She was doing it out of the goodness of her heart, not for a paycheck but right under my nose, she was steadily getting physically worse.

The good times couldn't last forever, could they? It was the calm before the storm. After the operation, the biopsy revealed that she had stage 4 cancer. They told us you don't get hip cancer so it had to have originated from somewhere else. They did a PET scan and found out she had stage 4 cancer of the lung.

All the money in the world couldn't bring my mother, Sarah, back or cure my birth mother's cancer. Even as I was sitting at Joan's funeral, my mind was struggling with so much loss. With Joan, it was sudden and smacked me right in the face, while Mary's cancer reminded me of Sarah's fight — slow and painful.

I was once again anticipating death and what it was going to be like. Not just for me but for her other children and her husband Lou.

I know in my heart that I wouldn't give up a moment of the relationship I had with Mary; but I also know myself well enough to know that there will be days that the pain is so devastating that I won't be able to bear it. There just isn't a word that explains the pain, and there is definitely no way to prepare for it.

The doctors told us Mary had only a few months to live, but we ended up having six great years before the cancer took her. Like myself, she was a fighter and

Mary and I Loved Traveling Together

hung on. Coincidentally, they also told us that Cherié only had months left to live, but she ended up getting three more years with us, so you never really know. No one can put an expiration date on a living thing.

For the first few years, Mary would spend half her time in Las Vegas and half her time in New York because her medical insurance was only accepted in New York. Even after two rounds of chemo and being on thousands of pills, she kept fighting. **She got dressed up every single day and tried to make the best of life.** We still made plans. We would go on vacations together and tried living life as usual. I felt if I kept her busy with things, she wouldn't allow herself to just sit at home and let the cancer overtake her.

Frank Marino

My 30th Anniversary on the Strip

In the middle of dealing with Mary's illness, my brother, Alan, started having severe stomach pains. He had just come to visit me for my 30th anniversary as a headliner on the Strip. Caesars Palace had given me the penthouse for my celebration. **Alan came in with my sisters, Nadine and Toni to help me celebrate this historic event.** (By this time both Sarah's and Mary's families had put their differences aside and just got along for my sake. Thank goodness!)

Shortly after that event, Alan went in to see a doctor about the stomach problems. He was instructed to go to the hospital for more tests where they told him that he had cancer. And the blows kept coming at me.

They told him that the cancer was too far gone so all they could do was make him as comfortable as possible, like a hospice situation and within days, he was gone.

Drags to Riche$

My Idea of Traveling Light

My Brother Alan with Me and Our Sisters

Alan was Sarah's biological son so he and I had grown up together from the time I was seven years old. He remembered that when my first mother Sandra Marino died and my father took me to Disneyland to help me through the pain. It's probably one of the reasons that Disneyland is still so special to me today. So much so that I go to one Disney park or another at least once a year.

I remember Alan as always being very strong and macho, sort of that typical New York Italian. I talked to him on the phone before he died that night. He had two young children and even though he was the kind of man that didn't cry, he was crying. **He asked me to do for his children what my father had done for me -- take them to Disney.** He was worried most about his youngest, Aiden. He'd taken his sons to Disneyland before but he felt that Aiden had been too young and might not have remembered it. This was his dying wish that he asked of me.

My Family at Disney World

I kept my promise, October of 2017, I took the entire family, not just his family, but my two sisters' families as well, to Disney World. We all celebrated in his honor. The kids had a great time and the families will always remember the good times that we spent together at Disney World.

Shortly after, Alan's passing **I went on a short tour with my show.** We played Niagara Falls, Biloxi, Mississippi, and I was on my way to Hawaii, the last stop of our "Divas" tour. I had just landed in the early morning when I got a call that my mother, Mary, was asking for me. Looking back, she probably knew her time was up. I had the entire cast and crew with me in Hawaii but I dropped everything so I could get to New York. I told the family that I was on my way, but, as it turned out, I couldn't get a flight until the next morning.

By the time I finally made it to New York, my mother Mary had passed. The last time I got to speak with her was a week earlier on the telephone for her 71st birthday. I remember telling her to hold on as after I was done with the tour I'd be coming to New York to visit with her. It's so strange that Sarah ended up dying before she could see my own show. **Mary got to see my "Divas" show but unfortunately, never got to see the "Showboy Mansion," completed.**

Do Everything You Can Today Because Tomorrow's Never Guaranteed

16

Knocking Down My Playground

It wasn't just people dying around me; one huge chunk of my past was dying as well. Once again, I was in bed one morning (and by morning I mean afternoon), when I heard the disturbing news that the Riviera Hotel had been sold. I was reading through my emails on my phone with the news on in the background when they made the announcement. Mornings are my time to wrap my mind around the day I have ahead. I always check my phone, the news, and my schedule. It's the way I wake

The Riviera Says Goodbye

up and get in tune with the world around me and the nights are packed with the glitz and glamour of my work. I normally fall into bed, exhausted after a full day around 2 or 3am, but from around noon until two I can peacefully get caught up on the outisde world before my "crazy" life takes over.

My Seamstress Mardy with Cherié

I need a reality TV show because I don't think anybody would believe how crazy my life is unless they saw it for themselves.

From the moment my day begins, everything becomes completely over the top. That particular morning I had a conference call with my publisher, followed by a costume fitting with my seamstress Mardy, a doctor's appointment, and a meeting with a production company — all interspersed with daily chaos. The chaos consists of emergencies — of which we have hundreds in any given day.

"Frank, we need you to sign this."
"Frank, will you talk to so and so?"
"Frank, someone wants to book you for…"
"Frank, are you busy…"
"Frank, could you…"
"Frank, so and so won't…"
"Frank, so and so called for some comp tickets."

I'm pulled in a million different directions and I think that's why I need that time in bed to prepare myself mentally.

Normally during my quiet me time in the morning, I'd only listen to the news with half an ear. That half an ear caught the fact that the Riviera had been sold to the Las Vegas Convention Center and that they were going to implode it to make room for a Convention Center expansion.

I dropped everything to take it all in. You can't work at a place like the Riviera Hotel and Casino for almost 25 years and not have the history of the place etched into your heart. I mean, for God's sake, I grew up in that building. **I was a little shaken at the thought of it being gone.**

The Riv, as we called it, was one of the last of the independently owned hotel/casinos on the Strip. It had been facing buy-outs for years and there was a time that the employees themselves bought shares to keep the Riviera out of the hands of Corporate America. They had one offer to purchase the hotel a few years before at a premium price of well over a quarter billion dollars, but now, after the bankruptcy, the board was only able to sell the hotel and property for about half of that previous offer.

Before it permanently closed, I went to the hotel and made the rounds. **I said goodbye to all the hotel em-**

Love Those Zebra Seats

ployees I'd worked with who were still there. There were still a few because the Riviera was a place where people put down roots. Everybody remembered me and it was like I'd come home. I talked to the long-timers in the restaurants, the casino floor, different porters who had worked up in the showroom areas, the valets that took my car every night, and front desk people. **It was really a touching experience. I even got invited to a going away party that the employees were going to have.**

After the doors finally shut, they decided to have an auction. I remember when they designed the showroom for "La Cage," it was modern and space-aged for its time. The chairs were done in zebra stripes. It was probably one of the most famous showrooms in town at that time because it was so avant-garde.

One Last Look at My Dressing Room

When you'd walk up the steps to the "La Cage" showroom you would see these **two grand hand-blown chandeliers that were amazing. They were very art deco and they were a piece of my history. I admired them every day that I went in to work.** To me, from the first moment I saw them, they stood for the glamour and elegance of the show I was in.

I knew everything was going to be for sale so I tried to call the liquidation company and tell them I wanted to buy those chandeliers from outside the showroom. They said those were the only things they weren't going to sell but **I didn't give up that easily.** I kept trying and trying. When the auction day finally arrived, I did go down and, much to my surprise, they had a price tag on them.

I said, "I want to buy these. You said they weren't for sale but there's a price tag on them!" They again refused to sell them to me and yet they were on the cover of the newspaper advertising the liquidation sale. I finally threw my hands in the air and set my sights elsewhere.

I ended up buying one of the neon art pieces from outside the front of the showroom with the famous "La Cage" feather on it. As soon as I got home I happened to get on Facebook only to discover that one of my ex-cast members attended the auction as well and bought the chandelier I had so desperately wanted.

I called the liquidators again. I just had to know what had happened. They said there was a mistake. I said you made the same mistake five times as I sat there on the phone balling them out — I was so mad. I was happy for my ex-cast member who'd gotten it but I was furious at the liquidators. Once again, I ran into people who didn't know how to do their own jobs. I had really wanted that chandelier as a memento of the time I spent at the Riv.

I had some of the best times of my life in that building. I was only 19 years old when I first arrived in Vegas, so I literally grew up there. To this day I'm still really good friends with Pia Zadora who had owned the Riviera for a period of time. Now she lives down the street from me, but at that time, she lived in the penthouse of the hotel. **How cool it must have been to own a hotel and live in it!**

Pia Zadora Backstage With Me

Frank Marino

The Good Old Days

It only seems fitting that Pia Zadora and I made plans to watch the implosion from a penthouse at the Turnberry luxury highrise condos which is right next door to the Riv. This particular unit belonged to the famous set designer and friend of mine, Andy Walmsley. Seeing it come down like that was like that moment in **"Planet of the Apes"** where Charlton Heston sees the Statue of Liberty buried in the sand and he knows in that moment that there's no going back. A piece of my history was gone in a flash!

I was also very shocked to learn that the new owners of the Riviera were just going to let my first star on the Vegas Walk Of Fame get blown up with the building. You wouldn't believe the angst of having to move one of these things, but I couldn't

The Riviera Implodes!

just leave it there. **Like I was going to let that happen?** I actually hired a company to excavate it and reinstall it at the entry gate of my new home.

But like Joan dying, the Riviera imploding closes yet another chapter of my life. There's no going back now. I have nowhere left to look but straight into the future.

If You Don't Step Forward, You're Always Going To Be in the Same Place

17

The Showboy Mansion: My Starter Castle

After all the deaths and the demolition of the Riviera, I decided to design and build something I always wanted... the Showboy Mansion. **The house I had been living in was the one I'd bought when I first came to Las Vegas.** I was 19 when I designed it and I'd lived there for over 30 years. I'd been there so long, they even named the street it's on Frank Marino Drive in my honor.

I think I put moving off not because I didn't have the money to go bigger, but because I knew that my next home would have to be my dream home, and nothing less would do. I'd always wanted a mansion and with all this death around me, I became motivated to check this off my bucket list.

I had actually started designing a completely different house. I owned a piece of land that I bought years ago. **I sat down with an architect and we designed what I thought was going to be my dream house.**

My Realtor and Good Friend Melanie

The week that we were to break ground on that house, my realtor, Melanie VanBurch, called me and told me that she found a house she thought I was going to love. I thought, "Ugh, I don't want to go look at another house. I had been doing that for the past 20 years. I'm ready to break ground — " Still I agreed to look.

It was a big but outdated mansion in the Eagle Hills Community in Las Vegas. The neighborhood was amazing and against my better judgment, I ended up liking it. I mean, I really liked it. Here I had a complete set of plans for my dream home and yet I still liked this one better? **Was I crazy?** Yes, it was old but I had a vision and something about it just spoke to me.

Alex, on the other hand, walked in, took one look, and walked right back out again. **He loved the neighborhood, but the house was like the Palace of Versailles and a rustic ski lodge had merged together and created one big, ugly mess.** It had all this marble and wood mix that just didn't go together — but I wasn't looking at that, I was looking at what I could do with it. Let's face it, I was going to put my magical touches on anything I decided to live in. I pulled Alex back into the house and started to explain to him how I envisioned it. When he got the feel for the place, and started to see my vision, he saw the house in a whole new light. Once the light clicked on for Alex, I knew this house was the one.

We called the contractors to stop the construction of the other house immediately, and that, my friends, was the beginning of many, many unforeseen headaches. I also was

Celebrating the Purchase of the Showboy Mansion

threatened by the architect/builder who was supposed to break ground the next day. He said if I wasn't going to build that house, I had to pay him $40,000 because he would have earned that money if he had built the house per the contract. Not only did I have to pay him off, but I had to sell the land I was going to build on. The bottom line was that Alex and I both liked the new one and that hadn't happened at any of the other places we had seen over the past 20 years. That made these obstacles all worth while.

The Plaque at the Entrance of Our Home Says, "And So the Adventure Begins"

We gutted the house, taking it down to the studs and foundation. I was so nervous because I couldn't see it coming back together. At this point, it started to seem overwhelming and I thought, "What have I done?"

It took two years to fully remodel it the way we wanted. In these years, we left a dumpster full of contractors, designers, decorators, and architects as they just didn't see our vision. The first contractor quit because he thought it was going to

Our Housewarming Party Wonka Style

be a piece of cake. **He didn't realize that when I said I wanted to redo everything, EVERYTHING included every darn thing in the house!** There would not be a single knob, tile, faucet, or fixture left from the current home. It ALL had to be redone. At first, he gave me one quote, but when I showed him what I wanted to do, he tripled it. **He looked at me. I looked at him and we both realized at the same time that this was way above his head, but it took him six months to tell me he couldn't do it.** He told me he wasn't feeling well, had back trouble and he didn't want to let me down and graciously resigned from the job.

Frank Marino

My Swirl Staircase

The Formal Living Room

The second contractor quit when I was bidding out the house to other contractors and he didn't want to compete, which is sad because he was the front runner. I found the final contractor through my investment broker, Mike Chudd. Jack Raferty was his recommendation and he's probably built half the mansions in Las Vegas.

At that point, the first decorator quit because he had an argument over Raftery being a take-charge kind of guy. **Suddenly my house was labeled by him as an "angry project."** He said he just couldn't work with such negative energy, so he resigned.

It didn't matter. I only got the decorator because Alex liked his work from a magazine. I didn't need a decorator! I was just using the guy to order materials I wanted and get a

Frank Marino

Disney Themed Movie Theater

My Formal Dining Room

decorator's discount from whatever contacts he had. I knew what I wanted in the house and I didn't really need any creative help. All I needed was Alex's opinion on certain things. I learned that decorators are funny. We'd hire one and they'd throw a creative temper tantrum and then bow out. It became a joke near the end. **I finally realized that they think that you're going to live in something they create with their tastes and really never respect your opinion.**

When we bought the Showboy Mansion for almost $2 million, the renovations were initially going to cost $495,000 however, the renovations cost closer to $4 million. When it was all said and done, it ended up costing about $6 million from concept to completion.

One example of how the costs kept adding up, was my realtor, Melanie, thinking that I could buy a toilet for $350. She had no clue. My master bathroom toilet ended up costing me $7,500! (Boy was she wrong!)

Even My Powder Room is Amazing!

We ended up picking every knob to every fiber of carpet. I learned drapes aren't just material, there's the rod, the fabric, the sheer behind the drape, the flow of material, and the beading on the fringe. There were a million tiny details to every decision that went into the house and I kept my eye on every last one of them.

The only original items that remained in the house are the rose bushes out back (they are gorgeous and still thriving today), the eight movie theater chairs, the garage cabinets and the three tubs in the spare bathrooms. Everything else was ripped out and replaced. I even added seven additional feet to the downstairs bedroom so that I could duplicate my old bedroom exactly like the one I had lived in for the last 30 years.

Now I Even Take the Trash Out in Style
With My Louis Vuitton Trash Bin

The Home Hair Salon

I even re-cut my old drapes to fit the new windows. This is in case one day I can't go up the stairs, I will just move in there. **With all the headaches I went through, I plan on this being my last house... EVER!!**

But, in the end, it was totally worth it. The Showboy Mansion is a one of a kind 15,000 sq. ft. home that has a Disney-themed movie theater, a full service hair salon, gift wrapping room, library, gym (just for show), two offices, a huge formal living room, dining room and a cathedral ceiling that rivals the Sistine Chapel!

In the formal dining room, I only use real silver flatware. I also have several sets of china depending on my mood. I change them seasonally and for the holidays. **I don't just buy**

My First Dinner Party

things and put them up for show, I want to use them and enjoy them every single day. I mean why have them if you're not going to use them?

My first formal dinner party was an Italian feast and it was the first time the stove got used since we moved in. Superstar Tony Orlando, his wife Frannie and daughter, Jenny, Pia Zadora, and her husband, Mike, Aunt Chippy (Jimmy Kimmel's Aunt), Melanie, and, of course, Alex. Everyone raved about the lasagna dinner that was prepared by my very good friend and personal concierge, Leah Koza. I like to entertain, and I do it often now, whereas before I never did. Holiday family dinners are now always at my house. That's the only time the stove/oven gets used. Thanksgiving is a buffet feast. My yearly Oscar

Alex, Neil Sedaka and Me

The Property Brothers

viewing party is a hard ticket to get. New Year's brunch is now a tradition. **The legendary Neil Sedaka even enjoyed playing on my white Steinway Grand Piano when he stopped by for lunch one day. Thank goodness the piano also plays by itself for the days when Neil can't make it over!**

I've had so many stars visit my home, I often wonder what the guard gate thinks when someone like

Mary Wilson, Priscilla Presley and Me

Oscar Viewing Party

Priscilla Presley gives her name to them or ever Mary Wilson from the Supremes. I even had the Property Brothers over who thought the house was simply amazing.

    I actually have a room just for gift wrapping. This was my compromise for Alex getting a movie theater. It was important to me because I love to decorate for the holidays so I needed an entire room, a place that isn't outside or in a garage to store the beautiful ornaments and decorations that I put on gifts. I spend lots of money, love, and energy on Christmas, birthday, and Halloween decor. No more dragging stuff out of the garage where it gets ruined. Now my bows and ornamental wrappings are pristine and ready for me in their very own room

My Gift Wrapping Room

and, for the same reason, my master closet has special area for all my Louis Vuitton luggage so it doesn't have to be stored in a basement or some out of the way closet.

Halloween is also always over the top in the Eagle Hills Community. We get over 2000 kids that trick or treat in our neighborhood. During the two years of construction on the house, we still handed out candy on the front porch. One pound candy bars are required to keep up with the other homeowners. Some of them hire food and ice cream trucks, and one neighbor even has an entire candy store setup. I now have to start upping my game. I think next year I'm going to put a small circus in my yard and have live animals. And since we're in Las Vegas, maybe I'll see if Cirque du Soleil can send over some acrobats.

Backyards are for Entertaining Too!

We've already had several magazine articles and television shows that featured our holiday decorations. They get bigger and better every year. **I have trees for Christmas, Halloween, birthdays, and even Valentine's Day.** They each have their own ornaments, ribbons, and decorations. I'm very big on traditional family values. As crazy as my life is, my home life is very structured. I think that I collect these items because of the joy they give me and also remind me of the personal struggles I had to go through to get them. I've lost three sets of parents, a brother, a mentor, and many friends and family members, so to remember them around the holidays brings a smile to my face and joy to my heart.

I must admit there are still times when I miss my old house because I'm really not good with change. I probably could have lived there forever but after 30 years, I really had outgrown it. Now after two years of blood sweat and money, the "Showboy Mansion" is no longer my dream house, it has become my home.

I Believe When You Invite Guests to Your Home, You're Inviting Them to Yourself

18

Reality Hits!

At this point, I've achieved most of my goals and dreams because I chased them tirelessly. I built my Showboy Mansion as well as a career as a Vegas Superstar, but now I set my sights on my own reality TV show. The first time I was introduced to reality TV was "The Anna Nicole Smith Show." I actually ended up becoming good friends with Anna before she passed. What a great lady! And then "The Osbournes;" I actually performed at Ozzy's 50th birthday party. The trend used to be talk shows then it went to travel channel specials, and now

With Anna Nicole Smith

it's Reality TV so if I could just get myself and my cast on television again, we would be standing room only every night.

Right now, I average around 600-800 people that come see the "Divas" show every night in Las Vegas. Since day one, I've greeted them outside after every show and sign autographs. Everyone raves about what a wonderful experience they had. I love to take photos with the fans and I listen to their comments and suggestions but I know I could touch so many more people through the power of television.

Me and Ozzy

Good Friend Theresa Caputo, the Long Island Medium

At this point, I've done over 300 commercials, selling everything from cars, shoes, and even patio furniture, as well as hundreds of talk shows, guest appearances on other TV shows and movies. It only makes sense to me that my own reality show is the next logical step.

Drags to Riche$

Recapping "Dancing with the Stars" with Dayna Roselli

Because my crazy, over-the-top day-to-day life is made up of stuff that no one would ever believe. For all the ridiculous things that go on in my life, there should be an Emmy on each side of my desk to frame out the Academy Award I hope to win someday.

Shooting Commercials

Signing a Celebrity Wall

I'm not the only one to think so because every television production company wants to do a reality show with me.

Because every time I'm a guest on someone else's show, like "Tia and Tamara," "Toddlers and Tiaras," "Tanked," "The Property Brothers," or "Long Island Medium," they get extremely high ratings. I've also been a guest on a lot of other types of television shows like "E!'s New Money" series, "Extra," "Entertainment Tonight," "Home, Strange Home," "Good Morning America," and so many others. I realized that these days, it's competition shows like "America's Got Talent," "American Idol," and "The Voice" that are what's making future celebrities. I personally don't believe that you can just add water and poof you're a star. I really believe that you've got to put in the time, hard work and face rejection to truly last in this business.

When I talk to the production companies, they love me. They always ask me to be a guest on their shows and I love to do them. Many of these production

Only I Could Make a Garage Sale Look Expensive

companies want a reality show focused around me and they seem to be 100% behind it. We've actually made over ten pilots with various titles like "Behind the Queens," "Wigging Out," "Frank My Way," and "The Real Headliners of Las Vegas."

Although, it always seems to fall apart at the network level like with **ABC, NBC, CBS, Bravo,** etc. I remember that all the networks did the same thing with my good friend RuPaul. A gay channel called Logo, which was on the verge of crashing and burning, took a chance on RuPaul and, in my opinion, he single-handedly saved that network with his "Drag Race" show. I'm so happy that someone was able to say, "I'll show you," and he did.

Filming a Commercial for Drag Race

Actually, RuPaul is my favorite female impersonator. I love his style, his look, and his music. Many of the cast from my show have even been guests on the Drag Race Show. Someone needs to tell these TV executives, **"This isn't England, there can be more than one Queen on television."**

Speaking of England, the inside scoop is that I just recently starred in a reality series in Great Britain called "Last Laugh in Vegas." I had gotten a phone call from Andy Walmsley, who you remember from Emmy-winning set designs on "American Idol." He told me that they were doing a new show about 10 older British stars who had done everything including performing at the Royal Albert Hall for Royalty but have yet to fulfill their final career dream of performing live in Las Vegas.

"For the finale," Andy tells me, "we want to get them their own big production variety show." **They needed a Vegas producer, someone who could groom them and show them what it takes be a real Las Vegas headliner. He wanted me to be this Las Vegas guru and Vegas-**

In Manchester, England, Taping "Last Laugh"

The "Last Laugh" Cast

ize them. Since Liberace was gone, I was the next logical choice.

Alex and I flew out to Manchester, England to meet them and begin the process. One was a piano player. One was a teenage heart throb. One was a pop star. Two were comedians. They were from all different genres of entertainment.

"Last Laugh" Finale

I had watched all their performances on the internet before I got there so I knew what I was walking into. Some of them had been to Vegas for a vacation over the past 30 years so they were familiar with my work as well.

When they came to Vegas, we put them in a house together and started their "Vegas" transformation. We took them around and introduced them to people they needed to know in order to fine tune their act for Vegas. **We then had a huge welcome party to show them off to all my famous Vegas friends. I coached them on every aspect of how to become a headliner in the Neon City.**

For the finale of the TV series we produced a true Vegas Spectacular and performed it at the Orleans Hotel where they were given a chance to show their amazing talents to an American audience. **At last a reality show that featured my talents! I was again the number one show on ITV1 it made me a household name in Great Britain,** however I still want a reality show of my very own here in America!

God Shave the Queen!

Baby and Angel

When my dog Cherié passed, I thought I wanted to die as well. After all, I didn't have any children so I felt like she was my child. I begged Alex not to get another dog, at least not for a while. I didn't feel it would be right to fall in love with a new puppy. **I felt as if it would be disrespectful to Cherié and her memory and I was afraid of the guilt I would have.**

Baby and Angel in Their Louis Vuitton Outfits

Alex and I Snuggled Up with the Kids

Although unbeknown to me, behind my back, Alex did go to the pet store. When I found out, I was mad, at first, because I wanted him to be as upset about losing Cherié as I was. Apparently, when he was there, he fell in love with a puppy almost immediately. After many discussions, **I finally agreed reluctantly to go with him to see this dog that I knew couldn't possibly be as wonderful as Cherié.**

When we showed up at the pet store, Alex showed me this little Bichon Frise puppy, a white ball of fur with attitude to spare. He was so adorable and when we turned to leave, the poor dog started to cry non-stop. Alex picked him back up and he finally settled down, but we eventually had to leave.

We didn't get the puppy that day, but we went back to see him again later that week. When we asked about him, they said that he was quarantined because he wasn't eating, and they wanted to see what was wrong. They felt it was separation anxiety because we had left him that day after playing with him. **Alex was beside himself.** We then came back the next day to be with him again. Every time he would put him down, he would cry more and more.

The Boys Waiting for Treats

What could I do? It would have been selfish of me to tell him that we couldn't get another dog. He deserved to have that same bond that I had with Cherié. But it hurt me to see it so soon and Alex knew it. So, Alex said, "Instead of getting another little girl dog, we'll get two boys," which is what we eventually ended up doing. So we named the first one Baby Boy because of his crying.

Then we were on a mission to find a second dog as well. We went to a million pet stores. Truthfully, I fell in love with every dog I picked up. Nothing is more gratifying than the unconditional love of an animal.

Frank Marino

Taking the Boys Home for the First Time

Baby and Angel's First Birthday Party

Cherié, you remember, was a Maltese breed dog so every time I looked at one, I would tear up. We finally found another little boy. He was a mixture of Maltese and a Poodle that they call a Maltipoo. I think Cherié smiled at us that day because we named him Angel. I still felt guilty over having these new dogs, but my heart opened a crack and they wiggled right in there.

At first it was a shocker. We were used to having one small female dog who was extremely well trained. Cherié knew exactly where the doggy doors were, what to do if she had to go out in the dog run, only ate when she was hungry, and was perfectly well-mannered. Now we have **two little boys, thick as thieves from the start, who have turned our home and our lives upside down with their mischievous ways.** They are both milk-white, so they blend into all our carpets and furniture so well that they've turned our house

Frank Marino

With Their Nanny, Judy

into a giant hide and seek game. I have security cameras all over the house and even with them zoomed into places, I sometimes can't see them hiding. At least our carpets used to be milk white. Puppies don't always know how to go outside to pee. Still, even though it's going to cost me the price of a small sports car to replace the carpet, **I still can't bring myself to ever yell at them** when they have an accident. I would just work harder with them and when they finally learn to pee outside, I figured we could change the carpets out then. In the meantime, the carpet cleaner comes every month to remedy the problem.

I'd forgotten how much work puppies could be. Alex and I would take Baby and Angel to training classes once a week and we also had trainers come out to the house as well. It's definitely a process to get dogs to understand what we'd like them to do. Cherié trained us, but boys are different, rowdier and more curious. We had crate-trained Cherié, but now I was too much of a softy. The boys have their own nanny, Judy, who comes over whenever we have to leave the house for more than a few hours. I even let the dogs up on the bed every night to sleep. So, I can wallow for a while in their affection and boy

was I lucky to have it. Just as I started to heal from Cherié's death; I was thrust into grieving yet another death, more like a murder, the murder of my career.

It was a good thing that I had this distraction of the boys. Otherwise, I'm not sure how I would have weathered the betrayal that was about to come. **I do remember telling God when Cherié first got sick if you give me just a little more time with her, you can take away everything I have, my fame and fortune etcetera.** We did end up getting three extra years with her and I guess maybe it was my time to pay the piper.

It's a Dog Eat Dog World.

Embezzled, Embarrassed, Extorted and Exonerated!

This next chapter contains my version of what happened behind the scenes of the "Divas Las Vegas" Caesars Entertainment debacle. At the end of 2017 and into the first half of 2018, Caesars Entertainment started moving our show times around, to accommodate a new act they found to perform alongside Divas in the showroom, and basically gave me the feeling that they wanted to move the show someplace and find something that was more appealing to millennials, even though they had just signed a brand new five-year contract that we were only six months into.

I've been in this industry over thirty-five years and trust me, I know the business inside out. Had they just been straight with me from the start, I could have easily moved to another casino, but instead they were throwing these odd hurdles my way like taking away most of my advertising in

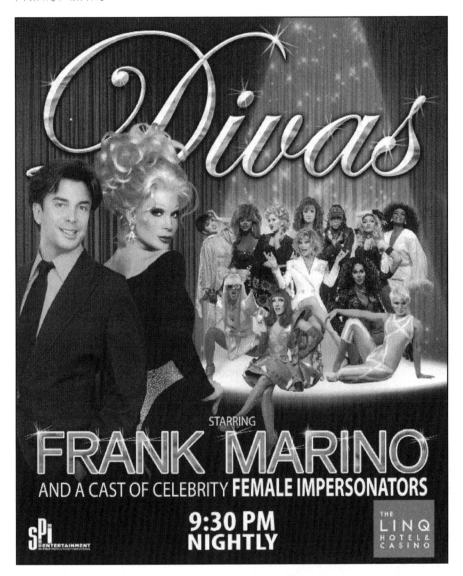

"Divas" Show Advertisement

the casino and giving it to the new show, renaming the showroom after the new act that was there thirty-five days not thirty-five years. And yet every time I jumped over one of their hurdles, the next one seemed to get bigger and harder. But, this was nothing compared to what was going to happen next.

I remember one meeting I had with the hotel, I was asked to make the show more like the Drag Race TV show which is the show RuPaul has on LOGO, the gay cable network I mentioned earlier, it is a contest type of show. I didn't see how I could make a stage spectacular work like a TV show which is what they were requesting, but **little did I know that they were actually in talks with that TV show already to bring their drag show to one of their properties!!**

Alex and I at My Celebrity Roast

Now before I dive into this chapter, let me take you back again to the early days of Divas. There was a well-known non-profit which will remain nameless that I donated money to. I also gave money to them from my side shows like my Celebrity Roast, which sold out the Stratosphere Hotel showroom as well as my appearance on "Conversations

Frank Marino

with Norm" which was at the Smith Center, a very elegant cultural theater for locals in Las Vegas. I had also set a precedent of sending them $200 every month just to be able to give back.

I would just write them a monthly check from a portion of my product sales. Just for the record, over the course of thirty-five years of performing in Vegas as the longest running headliner, **I can tell you I have donated money, show tickets or free personal appearances to at least 95% of all the charities in Las Vegas, which is why the accusations I was about to endure were so ludicrous.**

At one point, the charity informed me that they could no longer accept my monthly checks unless I signed a contract and filled out paperwork every time I wanted to donate money. I must admit I thought it was very weird that they wouldn't just take a check anymore. After going round and round, the person I talked to at the foundation told me I didn't have to do the paperwork every month, but that I could donate once a year and that way I could just do the paperwork then, at that time. I decided to just forgo the donations for a while because I barely had time to write the check itself let alone fill out paperwork.

One of the products that I used to sell was a $2 handheld fan that had the cast photo on it and said, "I am a Diva's fan!" It was a great promotional piece because, with Las Vegas heat, I knew that people would be walking around using them after the show. Around April of 2018, when Caesars moved my show from the evening time slots to a few daytime 4pm show slot, to me it made sense to start selling the fans again. **I figured that people get hot in the afternoon, so the fans would be a good thing.** After I'd been selling the fans for about ten months or so, I tried to contact the charity to tell them that I was ready to send them some money and fill out their paperwork. I called them three times and was put off three times. I just thought, "Wow, it's never been so hard to give away money," and I just couldn't send it as they told me not to years earlier.

On top of that, the beginning of June 2018, things started getting really crazy in my showroom. One day I came in and Caesars had fired most of their showroom cocktail waitresses, followed by the ushers, box office workers, and finally the maître de that had been there for almost forty years. Divas didn't have anything to do with that nor did I know why they fired all of them. When I asked about it, no one had any answers for me except that some Caesars employees might have been ringing drinks up wrong and possibly pocketing money. I'm not exactly sure and I really hate to speculate.

June 26th, 2018, I went on Facebook live before my 4pm show to do my new pre-show survey where I would let the audience pick which characters they were going to see that night which was a little thing I added to keep the show fresh. This pre-show kept my show unique as fans from all over the world could post comments. That night I remembered we got a few comments from Europe saying how they said they couldn't wait to see the show because they were fans of my reality TV show "Last Laugh in Vegas." **That evening we had a sold-out show to boot and also received a standing ovation.** I went outside, as usual to sign autographs and chat with fans as I always did. Then as I was heading back to my dressing room with my assistant, two of Caesars internal investigators stopped and asked if they could have a minute of my time. I said, "Yes, of course," and was taken to one of their conference rooms, supposedly to answer a few questions. But what started out as a few questions, ended up with wild accusations that started to fuel my temper. At that time, I found out that the non-profit hadn't called me back about sending them a check and filling out paperwork because **Caesars internal investigators had told them not to.**

While the investigators were investigating their own employees, I believe they said they had come to seventeen shows in which they had noticed one of my employees outside encouraging people to upgrade their seats for the price of $10-$20, in which you could actually be taken from the last row of the theater and put up front sitting next to someone who paid up to three times more for the exact same ticket. This program was designed to fill in any empty spaces up front and get a few last-minute dollars into the register. I had eight of the best seats in the house that I used for family and friends when they came out to see the show. When I didn't need them, my staff went outside and offered these upgrades to customers in line who didn't have great seats.

Earlier in the year I had learned that this employee was saying that a portion of the proceeds were going to the same non-profit that I was giving a portion of my product profits to. When I found out what he was saying, I immediately told him to stop, and I would constantly follow up to make sure he didn't start doing it again. Now don't get me wrong, I'm not the easiest person to work for and when upgrades were not doing well, I would ask him, "Who would not want to spend $20 to get a seat worth three times that much?"

The Divas Showroom

Frank Marino

He was probably using the non-profit's name as a way to get more sales. Something I've learned over the years of using the name of a charity is that only about one percent of the people buying souvenirs from the show do so because of a charity. Now this was a person who was not only my company manager, but also very close to me, so I was shocked to learn that not only hadn't he stopped using the charity's name but if he was paid in cash instead of a credit card, he would sometimes pocket the money and apparently split it with another employee. **The way they were able to do it and not get caught was, besides upgrading the seats I had allotted them, they would put in a pair of fake comp tickets which they were able to do because he was the company manager of the show.** So, while I was being interrogated in one room, he was apparently pulled aside and taken to another room where he admitted to this. When I found out what had been happening, I was totally heartbroken because I considered him to be one of my best friends, even family. He admitted it to the investigators that evening and that's also when I found out. He filled out an incident report that gave a step-by-step explanation of how he was able to pull this off. He also made it very clear that no one in the Divas show, cast or management had any idea that this was going on. I, of course, had to fire the two of them for embezzlement.

The Caesars Entertainment Department and I agreed that we'd take three days off and then regroup. I had to get somebody to do the company manager's job so that the show could run properly. **This incident happened on a Tuesday but come that Friday, they told me they decided not**

to continue the show. Their investigators had even said to me that they knew I had nothing to gain and knew I had nothing to do with it so the decision came as a shock. As with any business, had the money gone into the register, I would have gotten to keep it, so he was actually stealing from me, not them. But Caesars, for some strange reason, told me that I was responsible, as a vendor. I, being the boss, was responsible for all my workers, but what no one understood was that I was the person he was stealing from. This on top of losing my mother, my brother and my dog, I was heading for a breakdown.

The worst part was telling the cast and crew that they were out of work. These were people that I had worked alongside for a long time, some for up to thirty-five years. I took them out to lunch to break the bad news and tried to give them hope because I was contacted by some MGM executives to possibly move my show to the Mirage Hotel. I knew the head of entertainment there socially, but we'd never worked together before. I didn't tell them who I was meeting with, but I expected to reopen the show again the following month.

As fate would have it, I had to fly to Chicago that next evening with Alex for the Fourth of July holiday. **It was our twenty-sixth anniversary. I got on the plane thinking everything was going to be fine, but by the time the plane landed I went from a Las Vegas icon to the villain of the neon city.** The next thing I knew, a blogger said that I was stealing large amounts of money from a non-profit which involved sick children and their families.

Alex and I in Chicago For Our Anniversary

He made these wild accusations that, besides the money promised not going to a non-profit, he claimed that the show closed because of lack of ticket sales, which is absolutely ridiculous because we were working seven days a week because it was so busy. He was saying that we were constantly canceling shows, which was definitely not true because I have never canceled one show in thirty-five years except for those three days right after the investigation. He even mentioned that the hotel had wanted to get rid of the show, which I did not agree with at that point, because it didn't fit with the demographics that they were trying to attract. It wasn't until later that I realized that part was probably true.

I was livid. The fireworks for the weekend's Fourth of July celebrations couldn't compare to my temper. I ended up on every news program on every channel every hour on the hour and was the headline story in the Las

The Fireworks are Flying!

Vegas Review Journal for an entire week straight! Each accusation from the various media outlets was even more horrible and hurtful than the last.

Now because of all of this, the next day Caesars Entertainment changed their story and said the separation between Caesars and Divas was not a mutual agreement after all, as they previously reported in their press release. Now they were saying that the separation was strictly because of the situation with the non-profit. On top of that, with me being in Chicago and it being a holiday weekend, my lawyer was working overtime trying to talk to the charity so that we could make good on any of the money that my company manager said would be going to them. Remember, I had been trying to call them for weeks so that I could send them a check. But, I was told by the Caesars internal investigators that they were the ones that told them not to return my calls which is why I felt they were just trying to get rid of the show because had they just said to me, "Do you know about this?" I could have fixed everything immediately, which I actually did do the moment I found out what was going on.

    This whole situation had spiraled into a war against me on social media. I even received death threats on Facebook, Instagram and Twitter. People were going crazy commenting on what a horrible person I was. There were even cameramen outside my home, and I live in a heavily gated community. I was literally a prisoner in my own home. **A house that most people assumed that I bought with money I stole from the charity, which totally embarrassed and humiliated me.** I was told by my lawyers not to make any comments or statements, which I later regretted not doing because nowadays with social media being so strong, the game has changed and you're now guilty before proven innocent. I literally ended up going through all the stages of grief, anger, denial, guilt and acceptance. When I got to the point of anger, I started screaming from the rooftop, "How can you steal from a non-profit unless you work there? You either pledge to give them money or you don't." So, the people who were throwing stones at me obviously were people who probably never donated a dime in their lives. **It took every ounce of blood I had not to call these people ignorant, but I will do so now. They're ignorant.**

But nothing I did mattered. My silence in the press and social media only led people to say whatever they wanted, and boy did they fabricate some whoppers. The press started creating sensational headlines. It was hard seeing friends on the news or in the press talking negatively about me because I'd worked with these people in the media for so long during my career and they all knew what a loyal and generous person I was. I'd spent thirty-five years building my squeaky clean reputation, my show, and my career on integrity and sheer determination. It took only one false accusation to destroy it all.

And, in fact, at that point a lot of my cast also started turning on me as well. I quickly found out who my friends were. **I even lost my business partner, who gave over his thirty percent of Her-Larious Entertainment to me for free because he didn't want to be touched by the scandal.** But I feel Caesars screwed him as well. After recommending that he separate ties with me, because they felt they had proof that I was involved in some way, it ends up they had nothing, and in turn cost him lose lots and lots of money. They even went as far as to say that if they found that I was involved in the misrepresentation or pocketing cash from the selling of upgrades that he would have to fire my life partner, Alex, who as you know is the Vice President of SPI Entertainment. This definitely made life difficult.

On top of that, I lost a lot of endorsements both on televisions and in print, one of which was a Las Vegas Volkswagen company that had given me a cover-wrapped Volkswagen car to drive around in. The day after the incident happened, I received an email stating that with the closing of my show they would like to have their car back. I said, "No

Frank Marino

My Promo Car I Got From Volkswagon

problem, the car's parked out front with the keys in it. You'd better hurry and come get it before someone steals it." Little did I know that this was just going to be the beginning.

This is how I'm just like every other person in times like this. Big companies have the power and get to do whatever they like. **These bullying tactics continued. They made threats to "turn paperwork" into Las Vegas Metro, the FBI, the Gaming Commission, and even the IRS. Sounds scary, right?** Then I thought about it. I hadn't done anything wrong. I told them to do it. Turn in whatever they wanted. I wanted the vindication. I was tired of being browbeaten with insinuation and crucified in the press.

In turn, I decided to go overseas to one of the places that always cheered me up. Disney Shanghai had just opened so Alex and I hopped on a plane, but that ended up being a big mistake. It's a seventeen-hour flight, where all I could do was focus on all that happened and how I was wronged. If you've ever been in a situation where you've been unfairly blamed, you know that it's impossible to just sit for hours on end without having it torture you. The **unfairness of the accusations** kept pounding at me. All the Disneylands in the world couldn't

Trying to Enjoy Disney Shanghai

bolster me back up and then I had another seventeen-hour flight back home to sit and rehash it over and over again.

After returning home, I decided to hit the streets in search of work. I was not going to let the injustice be the death of me. After about a thousand meetings with various hotels, I got a green light from The Stratosphere Hotel and Casino for our show and entered into negotiations with them. They negotiated with me through a third party entertainment company for two and a half months which took me off the market but we had every detail taken care of down to how many towels each cast member would receive every night. After all that work they finally signed the contract and then fifteen minutes later my lawyer received an email saying that they weren't interested in having the show after all. Of course, after all this happened to me, it made me look even worse to not only the public but to all my cast members as well. After the scandal that just went on, it made it look like that's why the hotel didn't want us which had nothing to do with this at all. I honestly believe, after meeting the owner of the hotel, I felt maybe he was uncomfortable and for some reason just didn't like idea of a drag show in his hotel. The only satisfaction I got out of it was to find out months later that he lived in a home in the same gated community I live in. **It must kill him, this hotel owner and powerful businessman, to know he lives in a smaller house than the drag queen down the street.**

At this point, my confidence was so bruised I honestly didn't know if I was ever going to work again. This dragged me down into a deep, deep depression. It was so bad that there were times that I wouldn't go out of the house and wouldn't even think of driving my cars because both of them had personalized license plates. I became so paranoid, all I could think about was what people were saying about me. It was so bad that I had to finally see a psychiatrist who put me on antidepressants. I can truly say I wasn't myself at all. I can tell you that I would never kill myself, but I do now know why some people would consider it or even go through with it.

At this point, without having a job, every tabloid, newspaper and television news agency were still saying I was being investigated. **Yet again, I wasn't the one being investigated. The hotel was.** I had lawyers scrambling to be ready to deal with Las Vegas Metro, the District Attorney, and the Gaming Commission, only to have them make a few calls and find out that not one of those agencies was investigating me at all. It cost me $15,000 in lawyer's fees to learn from the Gaming Commission alone that I wasn't being investigated because nothing less than that would convince potential venues that nothing being said against me was true. All in all, I spent over a quarter of a million dollars total trying to clear my name of a crime I didn't commit.

The Truth Will Set You Free But First It Will Make You Miserable.

The Comeback is Always Better Than the Setback

Everywhere I turned, I felt like people assumed that I was the bad guy because of people not totally understanding the incident.

At one point, I went to Planet Hollywood to see a show with a celebrity friend of mine. I ran into the hotel manager of the LINQ, where Divas had been performing. I had a short conversation with her where I asked what she thought about the whole thing and inquired why she had never even given me a call. After learning that my employee confessed to the whole thing, she really had no answer. I just wanted her to know how sad and disappointed I was about the situation. Then, out of the blue about a month later, I got a letter from Caesars saying that I was no longer welcome on their property. Apparently, she must have complained about me confronting her.

Around this time, most of my cast were hired by a local hamburger restaurant which was going to let them perform. I was glad that they were getting work. Most of all, I wanted to make good by my cast. These were people that I felt responsible for and I was dragging myself to every venue I could find trying to get them back together and working. At one point, the burger place actually offered me a chance to buy into their business but when I went through their books, it just wasn't a good fit for me.

After leaving Caesars Entertainment, who own nine hotels on the Strip, and our meeting being politely postponed by MGM corporation, who owned ten hotels, there were only a few select hotels on the Strip left to apply to after the rejection from the Stratosphere Hotel and Casino. **The first one I went to was the SLS Hotel who, at first, seemed very interested.** They wanted paperwork from me stating that I was not being investigated by the Gaming Board and that I would have no problem with any agency if they were to hire me. They also wanted proof that everything was okay between me and the non-profit which I thought was crazy because the day after the story broke, they made a statement in the newspaper stating that they were happy with all the donations that I had made and how much they appreciate getting money from celebrities like me.

So after getting all the paperwork in order for SLS, I found the time slot they were going to give me was taken by another act. That being said, I recommended doing a Drag Queen variety brunch which is something that is really popular around the country these days. Again, I was jerked around and the next thing you know, they put another

Just a Brunch of Bitches!

drag queen brunch show in there instead. This time instead of feeling depressed, I started feeling determined to make this dark cloud go away. And by the way, that show closed after only five weeks.

I then went to the Golden Nugget downtown one evening for dinner. I was asked by so many people to take photos and give autographs that I thought maybe downtown isn't so bad. Maybe I should do a show down here. But, low and behold, I could never even get a return phone call from the person in charge. When I finally did, I was told the same old story that they were not looking to put in any new shows. Again, this only made me more determined.

My last shot was going to the Union Plaza which, in my opinion, is the tackiest and most undesirable hotel and casino in Las Vegas but at this point, I was desperate. They too strung me along for about two months telling me that they weren't happy with the show that existed there and if it were to close, they'd love to put Divas in. This also threw me off because this property was so bad that I thought that they should be kissing my ass to have a show like Divas in their showroom. That other show did indeed close and when we went back for the meeting, they too said they weren't interested in my show either. **To me that was the height of rejection.** This is a property that I normally wouldn't even want to walk into, let alone want to perform in their showroom but I was desperate. I would have done almost anything to be back at work.

The Christmas holidays came and went and I was almost to the point of giving up until one day when my assistant, Shawn and I went to have lunch at DW Bistro, a very hip and trendy restaurant which is owned by my good friend Bryce who asked me to do one of these Drag Brunches that I mentioned earlier. Of course, I said yes and put a show together for Super Bowl Sunday, which turned out to be amazing. This show was extra special. **My good friend, singer-songwriter Debbie Gibson told me she was coming to see the show and I asked her if she'd help me play a gag.** I said to her, can we play a joke and pretend I have a Debbie Gibson impersonator in the show but instead surprise them with the real one. To quote Debbie, she said absolutely, I'll be sure to bring my lashes and my high heels. What a sport. To have a celebrity of that caliber perform for us that afternoon. This is a lady who normally plays stadiums around the world. The show went so well that we agreed to do it quarterly. This was the first spark of hope that kept me going. I didn't even lose faith when one of my Divas cast members tried to put together their own show on the Strip without me. Of course, it ended up lasting only three and a half hours compared to my thirty-five years. Talk about fair weather friends. Some of my cast members decided to go with him instead of with me **but this time I got to have the last word and told them, "Now you've not only worked for the longest running headliner in Las Vegas, but you've also worked for the shortest one."**

With Debbie Gibson at the Diva-licious Brunch

I found out who my real friends are though. Tony Orlando, the world-famous entertainer, got me in touch with an agent who booked me and the Divas on a Florida tour in which we sold out every night in ten theaters that sat over 2,000 people a piece. That let everyone know, we still got it! We were also very lucky to sell out 400 seats in Vegas at the Italian American Club which was actually the launch of the tour.

Touring the World

Another old friend, a singer, producer and Cher impersonator, Heidi Thompson, suggested doing speaking engagements and that hit a nerve for me. I wanted to be able to tell my story and help others to know that no matter how bad their circumstances, they are not alone. I was thrilled to get a speaking engagement for a weekend in Dubai that actually paid $150,000 for two days work, which I thought was amazing. It's not like I was destitute or without options but I'll be damned if I let some bully make me go out on a bad note like this. **In the end, they'll be sorry they kicked me. They'll wish they'd killed me instead.**

So, speaking of death, before she died, Joan Rivers had once asked me while I was a guest on her TV show what I would do if she ever died. I quipped, "I guess, I'd have to join Legends in Concert." Ironically, that's exactly what I did do. For those of you who don't know, Legends in Concert is a live production show where tribute artists impersonate famous entertainers and performs nightly at the Tropicana Hotel and Casino in Las Vegas. My good friend, Mark Mercer, a top executive at the company, had called me up and asked if I'd be interested in working with them. I immediately said yes. I thought it was a great idea and agreed to a three-month contract which was great for me because I really needed, mentally, to go back to work on The Strip. The first night I went on stage, I said, "So, Vegas, did you miss

Discussing Dubai with Caroline Stanbury

Frank Marino

Becoming a Legend-ary Diva

me?" I was met with a standing ovation that reminded me that no matter how many times the big dogs knock you down, this underdog is loved by the people. And I must say in the midst of all this craziness it was the fans who never let me down, always asking when I was going to return.

Legends in Concert only booked me temporarily, at first, but they recognized a good thing when they saw it. To me, it was the perfect marriage. Las Vegas's longest running show and Las Vegas's longest running headliner joining forces at the classic Tropicana Hotel. And as of February of 2020, I became not only a permanent guest star of the show but received the longest and most lucrative contract Legends has ever given anybody.

So, what does it take to become a legend? I make this point because none of us ever know what's going to happen in life. I'd been to hell and back but I just kept fighting and just as my thirty-five year career was over in a flash, after fifteen months of agony, I was back on top just as fast. It takes getting knocked down and getting back up time and time again. **I became a Las Vegas Legend because I have determination and nothing will ever change that.**

There are a lot of important people who think they can control a person like me. They are wrong. They sit in their ivory towers and make decisions on subjects they know nothing about, but when it comes down to walking on stage, I'm the one with the standing ovations and they're the ones trying to figure out how to make their next buck. I'll take my applause over their approval any day. In the long run, I think I've beaten the big shots because I'm still standing, now on the Las Vegas stage, and forever as a Las Vegas Legend.

Frank Marino

After proclaiming that I had seen and done everything at the end of my first autobiography, His Majesty, the Queen over 25 years ago, writing that book showed me that it was only the beginning! My life was going to continue to be a roller coaster of ups and downs. I've been fortunate to experience things people only dream of -- being at the Tour de France in Paris, interviewing music's biggest stars at the Billboard Music Awards, Mardi Gras in New Orleans, the Kentucky Derby, Carnivale in both Venice and Rio, and traveling to every corner of the globe and, of course, coming home to the Showboy Mansion that rivals some of the best homes in the world. I've been blessed with such career highlights like getting two stars on The Las Vegas Walk Of Fame, a key to the Strip as well as a key to the city, a street named after me (which, by the way also goes both ways) and in Las Vegas, February 1st is considered Frank Marino Day.

Up to this point, I have triumphed over every obstacle thrown before me. I have legitimized an ancient art form that many who are ignorant of history still look down upon and I have made millions of dollars while doing it. No, I'm not bragging (ok, just a little) simply stating a fact. I guess I did, after all, like my reality show was titled, ended up having **the last laugh in Vegas!**

I've Truly Gone From *Drags to Riche$!*

The End... Or is it?

About the Author

Frank Marino has redefined the definition of a Las Vegas Headliner with his consistent 35 year reign as the Queen of the Las Vegas Strip. Marino is an accomplished author, comedian, fashionista, commentator, and one of the most famous female impersonators in the world as well as America's favorite male actress.

Marino is Las Vegas's most decorated entertainer. He has won numerous awards for his show "Frank Marino's Divas." He is now the star of the Legends in Concert show at the Tropicana Hotel and Casino where he performs nightly.

Marino is engaged to his long-time life partner, Alex Schechter, and they live happily with their two dogs, Baby and Angel, in the Showboy Mansion located in Summerlin, a suburb of Las Vegas.

Author's Final Note: As I finish this book, we are in the midst of a world-wide pandemic. Nobody knows if we'll be able to do the show ever again, but I guess the good news is that if you're reading this book, I was actually able to weather that as well.

My "Aha!" Moment With Oprah Winfrey

Get Your Copy of
My First Book at
www.FrankMarino.com

Follow Me On...

 Frank Marino &
Frank Marino Fan Page &
Frank Marino Divas Las Vegas
 @thequeenofvegas
 @thequeenofvegas
 FrankMarinosDivas

Made in the USA
San Bernardino, CA
17 July 2020